PRAISE FOR *LIVING IN GOD: CONTEMPLATIVE PRAYER AND CONTEMPLATIVE ACTION*

"This is an important book from a new author in the field. He faces directly the problem of trying to develop a real relationship with God and facing frustration when prayer and daily life do not hang together. Msgr. Amato teaches in simple steps how prayer and living in God's presence can develop into action. I found this book helpful and I am sure you will too."

-- Rev. Joseph Chalmers, O.Carm., Former Prior
General of the Order of Carmelites

"A very well done presentation of a way to achieve genuine union with the divine through the use of contemplative prayer. This approach should work well for those with a Christian background. It may also assist those of other faiths or no faith at all to achieve inner peace and a satisfying spiritual life, as they define it. The psychological insights and methodology provide a useful framework for anyone seeking a path to a deeper understanding of our fundamental unity with all of creation. Reading this book has answered some of the questions and overcome some obstacles I have had concerning religious approaches to living in and appreciating the present moment."

-- John of Doylestown, PA, a reader with no religious affiliation

LIVING IN GOD:
CONTEMPLATIVE PRAYER AND CONTEMPLATIVE ACTION

NICHOLAS AMATO

WESTBOW
PRESS°
A DIVISION OF THOMAS NELSON
& ZONDERVAN

WestBow Press books may be ordered through booksellers or by contacting:

WestBow Press
A Division of Thomas Nelson & Zondervan
1663 Liberty Drive
Bloomington, IN 47403
www.westbowpress.com
1 (866) 928-1240

ISBN: 978-1-5127-5425-4 (sc)
ISBN: 978-1-5127-5426-1 (hc)
ISBN: 978-1-5127-5424-7 (e)

Library of Congress Control Number: 2016913778

Print information available on the last page.

WestBow Press rev. date: 9/27/2016

DEDICATION

This work is dedicated to Abbot Stan Gumula, O.C.S.O. and the brothers of Mepkin Trappist Abbey in South Carolina. It is where I fell in love with silence many years ago, initially as a member of their monastic guest program, and it is to where I return to lead three Lenten and three Advent retreats each year. It is such an honor to be an associate member of this community of brothers, to share the life of the enclosure, and to be nurtured on the daily prayer, *lectio,* and good works of the monastery. It is a joy to know that one day it shall also be my final resting place.

ACKNOWLEDGEMENTS

Sincere thanks to those who have participated in the retreats I have had the privilege of leading over the years and who appreciated the many handouts, responded in myriads of emails to the workings of the Spirit within them during those days together, and who often suggested that I someday write a book on what was being presented. It has been your gentle urgings that brought me to this writing.

The five readers of the manuscript (Msgr. Ed Arsenault, Father Joe Chalmers, O.Carm., Nancy Reitz, John Sandy, Cindi Stewart, and Maureen Yantz) offered me alternate ways of saying what often seemed nebulous. Their constructive criticism and commitment helped me improve the several drafts through which this work has come.

To Margaret Benefiel, Executive Director of the Shalem Institute, and the Shalem staff especially Tilden Edwards, Ann Dean, Liz Ward, Carole Crumbly, and to the members of the Shalem Society, I am grateful for their inspiration and example to follow the call that comes out of contemplative prayer.

Finally, my deep appreciation goes to Maureen Yantz who served as both a reader and administrative assistant in getting the final manuscript to the folks at WestBow Publishing. She seemed never to tire of finding just one more thing to tweak, one more fact to check, one more procedure to refine, one more way of improving a figure. She was always there at my right hand.

PREFACE

This work could be seen as the fruit of my years leading retreats for priests and religious, as well as laity and clergy of many differing traditions. In many cases, its figures, appendices, and bibliography were the resources developed as handouts and reference points for participants. Its content was often the give-and-take of the discussions in session and in the private individual conferences where participants were seeking spiritual direction or discernment of how God was working in their lives.

Two sources contributed to its conception: the request from many participants to put the retreat into book form, as well as the desire to have a resource that anyone interested in the topic might access. Initially, a video interactive format was chosen that included webinars and podcasts. The implementation of this format did not prove as popular as was first expected, so the suggestion to write a book began to loom large.

In determining what format such a resource might take, it was clear that I would attempt to copy the format of retreats (namely, instruction, experience, reflection, and journaling) as closely as possible, given the limitations of the written word. Thus, the book does not read as a theoretical speculative work, but more as a workbook with some explicit exercises. It is a work calling forth your own experience of prayerful presence, reflection upon it, and then some writing or journaling. Only time will tell how successful I have been in achieving this end. Comments or questions are most welcome, for I see it as a work in progress. I can be contacted at fathernicholasamato@gmail.com, through my blog: fathernicholasamato.blogspot.com, on my Facebook page: Father Nicholas Amato, or on Twitter at @FatherNicholasA.

INTRODUCTION

If you are looking for a scholarly work, this book may be a bit of a disappointment, but if you want a concrete way of disposing yourself to experiencing God as face-to-face, to have that presence have an impact on your life, then this work may be of assistance. It has been composed with that goal in mind. I must quickly add that it is nothing we do to make that presence felt, for it is God's grace and desire to be one with us that brings it about. It is the abiding presence that Jesus calls us all to experience.

The present work is born of my own personal journey in responding to a yearning I was able to feel as a youngster, but never able to name. It continued to grow but was only contacted in deep moments of silence, sitting at my desk or wandering through the woods. It meandered through high school and college studies, dating, and career choices, yet it still remained just a feeling without explication. It was there, in the decision to study for the Catholic priesthood and in the tears, as my hands and those of Bishop Joseph Gossman were joined together, promising him and his successors obedience as a priest of the Church of Baltimore.

Fast forward 38 years to Mepkin Abbey in South Carolina and three months of silence, five and a half hours of daily community prayer, and weekly spiritual direction with Father Guerric, O.C.S.O., and the "feeling" began to take on words. Yet, at that time Father Guerric's words were, *"Nicholas, you came to the monastery with three things you might do in terms of ministry and are leaving with seven. I suggest you do nothing and simply dispose yourself to God's presence, and God will lead you. When it is time, you will know what to do.*" True to form as an extroverted thinker, I wanted to run with the excitement of an idea that suddenly comes into focus. But slow down I did, and within three months of prayer, what bubbled to the surface was to request Cardinal O'Brien, then Archbishop of Baltimore, to leave parish ministry and commit myself to full-time contemplative ministry. The yearning now, not only had words, it also had clearly become a ministry.

This book is the fruit of the years in the vineyard of God's dwelling with people who likewise yearn and long to see God's face.

CONTENTS

APPENDICES

FIGURES

CHAPTER

INTRODUCTION TO CONTEMPLATIVE PRAYER

A CONTEMPLATIVE LONGING

He was only 13, and while rather outgoing for a teen, he looked forward each day to coming home from school and sitting alone, deep into the field of cattails that bordered the back yard of the family's little three-bedroom ranch-style home. He'd sit for long, quiet stretches, gazing into the myriad of green stalks that drew him deeper and deeper into that field, and then he'd become lost as time stood still. Those were the first times he could name it, the longing he had to be in union with something so far beyond him, something he wasn't able to experience anywhere else. At times he was labeled a daydreamer, and while he wasn't sure what that meant, it didn't sound positive. No matter! His silent times were sought and treasured.

They call such events spontaneous spiritual experiences, and they come in a variety of shapes and sizes: resting in a sunset, holding a newborn, gazing at a field of sweet corn or sunflowers, watching a seagull or eagle glide, or being mesmerized by a trickling stream as leaves float by. As varied as they can be, they hold one thing in common – they take us deeper into a level of reality that is beneath outward appearances, and in the moment they feed and nourish a deeper part of who we are. They seem to touch our very soul. Thus, there is a feeding, a resourcing that ripples into who and how we are in the present moment, and we can come out of the reverie as if touched by grace.

The idea of such spiritual experiences - how we might dispose ourselves to enter them, how to remain there for longer periods of time, reflect on them, and put them into action - is the topic of this work. It is borne of those early childhood experiences, nurtured by years of contemplative prayer practices; a teacher's attempt to clarify, confirm, and demonstrate to his middle school children; and finally, as a priest to his people - how they, too, might enter the process and reap the amazing fruits of such a presence. Entering the process can be as natural and familiar as satisfying a summer's thirst with a frosty glass of lemonade and getting lost in the beads of water on the glass, or fulfilling a wintery evening's hunger with mom's meatloaf, mashed potatoes, and brown gravy.

There is a similar appetite within each of us for the divine. I like to think that God - before sending us out into the world through the birth canal - implants within us a longing for his presence. This is done to assure that we will more easily find our way back to him, which, of course, is the destiny of each of us. Let us be clear, no one returns by a straight line; not even the greatest saints among us. Instead, the return is circuitous, filled with dead ends, false turns. We are often retracing our steps over the same territory several times. I like to think of it as being similar to the GPS lady who says in a non-judgmental tone, *"Turn left at the next intersection."* Of course you say, *"No! I'm going to turn right."* She then comes back with, *"Make the first legal U-turn,"* to which you respond, *"No, I'm going to go left,"* to which the screen on your dashboard reads, *"Reconfiguring."* The fulfilling of the longing of our heart is never a straight path back to the Lord. The good news, however, is that different paths arise based on one's gifts and talents, one's character and tastes that are moments of partial fulfillment of this longing. The paths may be walking in nature, humming a song, gazing at an icon, reading a poem, sipping the first steaming cup of coffee in the morning, or watching a hovering humming bird at the feeder. The list is lengthy, but the result is the same; namely, that the longing for something deeper, something that satisfies, is to some degree fulfilled.

There were other touchstones along the way that brought me to a deeper sense of presence. As a child, it was my short-lived experience at being an altar boy. In high school, it was being in a service club called the Key Club. In college, it was having my own copy of *"The Imitation of Christ"* and finding little jewels on each page. Gradually, the longing drew me more deeply into Centering Prayer.

THE NATURE OF LONGING

There are few experiences more enduring or influential for the way in which we think about ourselves and the nature of our existence than our longings. They are in many ways the hidden core of our identity - that which informs our hopes and dreams, what rouses us to action. At the same time, they are somehow secret and precious to us, worth more than any amount of lucre or gain. Even though our longings can inspire feelings of dissatisfaction or pining, very few among us would be willing to trade the feeling our deepest longings arouse for any determinate ease or satisfaction. Yet, despite their importance and influence, they remain one of these least understood elements of human nature.

A longing is more than just a desire. One may *desire* to own a Mercedes Benz, but one *longs* for his/her mother's meatloaf, gravy, and mashed potatoes. What might be the difference? It seems that longings are cravings for something that was once possessed, whereas a desire can be for something that has never been experienced. With this in mind, it seems appropriate to conclude that the God for whom we long – *"As a deer longs for flowing streams, so my soul longs for you, O God,"* [1] – could be the inspiration and

---

[1] Ps. 42:1 (New International Version).

source of this longing. With the psalmist we could attest, *"You alone created my inmost being. You knit me within my mother's womb."*[2] If God loved us before we had a face, this same God would have planted such a longing within us in order to have us return to his presence daily and one day, forever. Longing then could be compared to an appetite, as thirst is to water, hunger to food, fatigue to rest. St. Augustine captured it in a timeless way: *"You have made us for yourself, and our hearts are restless, until they can find rest in you."*[3]

BEHOLDING

Combine this longing and the gazings of a young boy, and you begin to see the foundation for contemplative practice. This gazing, through the portal of nature or imagination, made possible an integration of passing insights and momentary deeper awareness - awareness beyond ego and the distractions of daily living. We might call such experiences mystical as in, *"Having a spiritual meaning or reality that is neither apparent to the senses nor obvious to the intelligence."*[4] More important, however, may be *"The individual's direct subjective communion with God."*[5] For some, it might take a thunderbolt or a voice from heaven, as it did for St. Paul on his way to Damascus. For others, it might simply be being open to the experience of oneness with all creation and oneness with God. For most, it seems that the conversion begins in contemplative presence and ends in action. Whether that takes place instantaneously, as it did with St. Paul, or if it will require longer – if not life-long practice – will depend on the individual and God's grace.

An easy way to enter such presence is to choose an ordinary object,

---

[2] Ps. 139:13.

[3] Dan Graves, "Our Hearts Are Restless" Article 15 *The Stories behind Memorable Sayings in Church History*, www.ChristianHistoryInstitute.org, (October 23, 2015).

[4] Merriam Webster, s.v. "mystical," accessed October 24, 2015, http://www.merriam-webster.com.

[5] Ibid.

such as a tree, candle flame, or household plant and simply relax into a quiet observing of it. Whenever analysis, judgments, or labeling present themselves, let them float by and simply return to observing what is before you. Allow your senses – each of them – to register aspects of the object: its shades of color, texture, movement, sounds, or even taste. Continue to return to the object whenever distracted or your mind takes you away from it. Gently blink your eyes, each time softening them a bit and begin to see what is beyond sight. Become aware of a deeper enfolding presence, a sacred union of you and the object and through grace. Should you return to the object, have an intention to deepen your presence to it - a presence that is beyond the material before you. Relish and savor that presence. Rest in it.

As we live each day, we tend to live unreflectively, almost zombie-like, having no real connection between who we are and what we are doing. It is akin to the drone on a bagpipe - just one long continuous low sounding note. Just as music needs both a variety of sound and silence, so our lives need space and a conscious recognition of diversity. Prayer, and especially contemplative prayer, is where we find this experience. We need to be awake, conscious, self-reflective, and taking in what is taking place in the rests between beautiful sounds (notes). How different it would be if we could accustom ourselves to say, *"Just this; this is enough. Let me take it in. Let me savor and relish it."* I am doing this as I write in my sunroom, looking at the wind relentlessly stripping the last leaves off the trees. They are holding on as if for dear life. Yes, that is "just enough." I need to remind myself that it is in the gaps and noticings of the diversity of my day, moment by moment, that God speaks most poignantly. It does take beholding.

SPONTANEOUS SPIRITUAL EXPERIENCES

Spiritual writers, James Finley among them[6], often speak of *"spontaneous spiritual experiences"* as moments of transcendence, moments when an object of beauty is beheld, and subject and object are one. Depending on the sensitivity of an individual, his or her ability to see beauty in the simplest of things and taking the time to notice - such experiences can be numerous even in the course of a single day. The more one feels gratitude for such experiences, the more one will experience them. A second effect of the gratitude is that you begin to experience them in the moment they are happening rather than only in the recollection of them. This doubles and triples the joy of living in the moment. This also increases the motivation to live this way with greater frequency.

LOOKING BACK AT THINGS BEHELD

There is a way of looking back to capture moments when we were in contact with deeper levels of reality, where deeper longings and beholdings met for a moment, but were not reflected upon. In her book, *"Journal to the Self,"[7]* Kathleen Adams offers 21 ways to recapture such moments through the practice of journaling. She is a student of Ira Progoff and offers creative ways for one to journal. One she calls *"Stepping Stones,"[8]* where the reader lists steps in the past that were important markers in his/her prayer life. Such events would be those that constituted moments that can be perceived as a shift in consciousness or direction. Recalling them helps us recognize deeper goals toward which we are moving either implicitly or explicitly. See Appendix A: *"Stepping Stones"* for the

---

[6] Finley, James. "Transforming Trauma: Exploring the Spiritual Dimensions of Healing," Gerald May Seminar, Shalem Institute, Rockville, MD, April 24-25, 2015.

[7] Kathleen Adams, *Journal to the Self,* (New York: Warner Books, 1990).

[8] Ibid., 48, 9.

survey. Thus, steppingstones from this perspective are moments when we became aware of prayer and realized a new way of thinking and relating to it. For example, my earliest steppingstone may have been my grandmother walking around the house with rosary beads in hand and the silent words of the Lord's Prayer on her lips, or the candle that burned before a statue at home, or my First Holy Communion Day. They are simply the markers that are significant to you as you reconstruct the movement of what would one day become your prayer life.

THREE KINDS OF PRAYER

Because I am writing for men and women of all faiths and all of whom are endowed with this longing, I want to acknowledge three forms of prayer that address this appetite. Each is uniquely different from the other. The goal of each of the types of prayer is the same - to experience the presence of God. In figure #1, we see the formats for each type.

Approaches Within Each Type of Prayer

The first, verbal/vocal prayer is the most common and involves thinking and speaking. It takes many forms: private and public. The second is meditation, where we may enter a scene of the Gospels or other source and imagine ourselves in it. Using all our senses, we engage ourselves fully in it. We recreate the scene, calling to mind what we see, smell, touch, and feel as Jesus singles us out and engages us. So, if it is Jesus looking up and speaking to Zacchaeus in the sycamore tree,[9] we become Zacchaeus, and he invites himself to dine with us. Here all the senses are engaged, the mind is thinking, and the imagination is fully engaged. We can feel the joy of the encounter. The final format of prayer is contemplation or contemplative presence. This form invites us to dispose ourselves simply to be in God's presence, where the disposing has to do with quieting the mind and freeing it of thinking and distractions,

---

[9] Luke 19:1-9.

and to have it simply rest in awareness. Rene Descartes, the 17th century philosopher, may have gotten it wrong when he declared, *"I think therefore I am."* Contemplation assures us that there are deeper levels of human "be-ing" than the ability to think. Awareness is a special place of presence, for in awareness, one is receiving the fullness of what is being presented and not participating in a reality that is circumscribed by one's ability to imagine or one's creativity. The question that arises, then, is how does one dispose oneself for such awareness? This will be the subject of our next chapter. For now, the testimony of several mystics regarding what is in store in silence and with awareness, should whet our appetites.

> *"God is more intimate to me than I am to myself."*
> St. Augustine[10]

> *"My Me is God, nor do I recognize any other Me except my God Himself."* Catherine of Genoa[11]

Effects of Each Type of Prayer

When one prays verbally or vocally in community, the mind is actively reading, processing, drawing meaning out of written symbols, and speaking them out loud. If the prayer is praise, God is offered glory and we are fulfilled. If it is intercessory prayer, then a request is made and we await a response. If it is contrition, we confess and are assured our sins are forgiven. Each verbal/vocal prayer relates to an expected effect or response.

In meditation, it is as if one moves from the orchestra of the theater

---

[10] St. Augustine, *Confessions of St. Augustine*, (New York: Doubleday, 1960) book 3, chapter 6, section 11.

[11] Richard Lang, "Being God," *Tradition*, http://www.headless.org/Biographies/st.catherine-of-genoa.htm, (October 25, 2015).

to the stage and becomes one of the actors in the play. The characters are interacting with me physically and emotionally. I become the character in the parable or the blind Bartimaeus talking to Jesus, and more importantly, Jesus is talking to me. The effects of meditation have to do with a visceral, tangible impact that the interaction is having on me. There is no waiting for a prayer to be answered.

Different in effect from the first two, contemplative prayer has God acting primarily, with us being present as fully as possible to receive that presence. The only "work" we are doing has to do with disposing ourselves to the divine, so God as light, warmth, truth, or love, may be both manifested and received. The effect is more of an afterglow - a radiance flowing from something beyond, yet within. It is described in the Gospel story of the Samaritan woman at the well[12] as living water, up from within, and its source is being in the presence of Jesus in faith and love. This grace is experiential, and the only prayer that is voiced may be a word or two that is soon dropped in order to move us from thinking to awareness. It may be that the word is recalled when we are distracted or begin thinking. The only wish we have is to rest in God and let God do with us whatever God would do. It is in the afterglow that grace becomes incarnate and operative in our lives as an effect of contemplation.

LEFT AND RIGHT BRAINS

New studies in brain physiology and how the brains of contemplatives differ from those who are not are many. Our brain's right hemisphere controls the muscles on the left side of our body and the left hemisphere, the muscles on the right side. So, in bending a finger on our left hand, it is our brain's right that is accomplishing the task. It is for this reason that in strokes or trauma affecting one side, the opposite side of the brain

---

[12] John 4:1-26.

will be manifested. Distinct from this, the left hemisphere is dominant when it comes to language and is also responsible for logical thinking. It is your left hemisphere at work when you are accessing facts from memory. The right hemisphere, on the other hand, deals with spatial reality and the arts. All that said, the brain balances and assigns control of certain functions to each side in order to ensure that tasks are divided up as a way to maximize efficiency. *"Brain asymmetry is essential for proper brain function,"* professor Stephen Wilson of University College London told Live Science. *"It allows the two sides of the brain to become specialized, increasing its processing capacity and avoiding situations of conflict where both sides of the brain try to take charge."*[13]

As brain activity relates to the three types of prayer, it is safe to say that verbal/vocal is focused in the left side of the brain where logic and language are at play, while meditation includes some right brain creativity and expansive imagining, as well as some left brain thinking. Contemplation, because it uses a word or mantra and then releases it to move to pure awareness or a resting in God, would be considered right brain activity, for while the goal is to eschew thinking, there is still cortical activity as awareness.

BRIEF HISTORY OF CONTEMPLATIVE PRAYER

Most people who are believers in God practice some form of verbal/ vocal prayer. Far fewer practice meditation, and relatively few have encountered contemplative prayer. All three forms are part of the Judeo/ Christian tradition from our earliest years. Jesus himself practiced all three. He prayed at home with his parents and in the synagogue on the Sabbath. He offered a reflective meditation to his listeners in his use of parables and stories of lost coins, lost sheep, lost children, vineyards,

---

[13] Robert Roy Britt, "Left vs. Right: Battle in Brain Discovered", January 22, 2009, *http//www.thinkproductiveusa.com*, (October 20, 2016).

and soil types. We know from the Gospels that he often went off by himself to be alone and in union with the Father. It is important to note that the Lord used this form of contemplative presence, where he simply rested in the Father's abiding presence before any big decisions were made. So, before his public ministry was to begin, Jesus spends 40 days in the Judean Desert. He leaves crowds of sick to go off by himself to be with the Father. He prays this way before setting his face like flint for Jerusalem, where he knows he will die, and again in the Garden of Gethsemane. What characterizes this contemplative prayer, but awareness, silence, being in the presence? It is out of this deep communion that Jesus draws the strength and determination to do the will of his Father. One has only to look at individuals who practice contemplative prayer to see the motivation that such presence and union can have in swelling one's spirits to live with a greater sense of love and compassion.

Contemplation has a long history as a gift from God for which we can prepare but cannot do for ourselves. Its earliest beginning is found in Jesus and continued to flourish in the early Desert Fathers and Mothers, in Celtic Christianity, and in the Churches of the East. From these early beginnings, such individuals as Dionysius and John Cassian taught it in the monasteries of ancient Christian communities. In the sixth century, contemplative prayer was codified into a monastic rule by St. Benedict between 530 and 560[14] and can be found in the unknown author's *The Cloud of Unknowing*. Contemplation continued to be taught and practiced by the Benedictines and by the Cistercian Reform of the Rule of St. Benedict in the 12th Century. The early Franciscans, the Dominicans of the Rhineland, and the Carmelites continued the tradition and built on it. In the 16th century, both Teresa of Ávila and John of the Cross, as Carmelites,

---

[14] The rule depends on preexisting rules and traditions from the 4th century. Among them are the rules and writings like St. Pachomius, St. Basil, St. Augustine and Cassian. Benedict's biggest source is one called *The Rule of the Master*, which was written several decades before his own and from which he copied extensively.

taught contemplation at a great cost to their own lives, for the Inquisition was raging throughout Spain, and individuals advocating or practicing this "new way" to pray were in grave danger. Thus, it was not so much that contemplative prayer was being taught, as that it was practiced and encouraged quietly, that carried it as a form of prayer through the Dark Ages and Medieval Times. The practice of contemplative prayer began to wane in the bloodbath that was the Protestant Reformation and the suppression of monasteries. The over-rationalization of the 17th and the 18th century Enlightenment had its part to play in the diminution of this third form of prayer. In the Counter Reformation of the mid-1500's[15] and the creation of seminaries with the Council of Trent, the verbal/vocal and meditation forms of prayer survived, but contemplation came to be referred to as "Mystical Theology" and, while it was taught, it was not encouraged or practiced. The situation would be akin to learning about the Feast of Christmas in a comparative religion course but not celebrating it with food, song, and worship. Most priests, and therefore Catholic Christians, were educated in this manner up until the reforms of the Second Vatican Council in the 1960s. Thomas Merton, a Cistercian (Trappist) monk, who died in 1968, was a central figure in bringing Western Christendom back to our contemplative roots. William Menninger, Basil Pennington, and Thomas Keating, all Cistercian monks at the St. Joseph's Abbey in Spencer, Massachusetts, set about responding to Vatican II's call to renew the contemplative tradition.[16] That was the beginning of "Centering Prayer," a term coined from the writings of Merton where he

---

[15] The Counter-Reformation, which was a type of Catholic Revival, saw a period of Catholic resurgence that began with the Council of Trent (1545–1563) and ended at the close of the Thirty Years' War in 1648.

[16] The Second Vatican Council was a worldwide effort on the part of the Catholic Church to address its relation to the modern world. From 1962 to 1965 the bishops of the world met at Saint Peter's Basilica in the Vatican. Changes resulting from the Council included the renewal of religious life, ecumenical efforts and dialogue with other religions, and especially for our purposes, the call to holiness that included everyone. Thus began the interest in the long neglected contemplative way to pray.

describes contemplation as, *"The awareness and realization, even in some sense experience, of what each Christian obscurely believes: 'I have been crucified with Christ and I no longer live, but Christ lives in me.'*[17] *It is awakening, enlightenment and the amazing intuitive grasp by which love gains certitude of God's creative and dynamic intervention in our daily life."*[18] *"It is not we who choose to awaken ourselves, but God who chooses to awaken us."*[19]

Response to the Trappists' initial work was very positive. Up to this time, believers had been leaving Christian Churches for Buddhist monasteries and Zen workshops. Transcendental Meditation was flowering. With a resurfacing of our contemplative tradition under the banner of Centering Prayer in the 1970's, Christians were able to find a form of prayer that satisfied their deepest longing and complemented and completed verbal/vocal prayer and meditation. John Main, an, English Benedictine (1926–1982), popularized this experience for ordinary folks by reintroducing the use of the mantra from teachings of the desert monks. He offered the laity an answer for living a deeper spiritual life and recommended two daily periods of such prayer, integrating them into the usual practices of Christian living.

Richard Rohr speaks of how, even apart from formal contemplative prayer practices, many may come to contemplation:

> *Many have always come to the contemplative mind as the fruit of great suffering or great love. These are the quickest ways to destabilize the self-referential ego. Those transformed by life and grace find themselves thinking simply, clearly, and in a non-argumentative way, without recognizing how they got there. They come to enjoy God, others, and even themselves,*

---

[17] Gal. 2:20.

[18] Thomas Merton, *New Seeds of Contemplation*. (New York: New Directions Books, 1961), 5.

[19] Ibid.

and do not need to pick fights in their minds about everything.
It is such a pleasant way to live! [20]

THE CONTINUUM TODAY

Today contemplative prayer practices are flourishing. It appears that there are three notable formats that are present for individuals wishing to respond to the longing within them for a direct experience of the divine. At one end, let us call it maximalist in that it offers the most complete presentation of the matter, is *lectio divina*, literally "divine reading." At the other end is Centering Prayer. Somewhere between the two is what one might call "the phrase that shimmers." Very briefly, *lectio divina* speaks of four steps to encountering the presence. *Lectio divina* describes a way of reading Sacred Scripture where you let go of any agenda and open yourself to God's presence. The first stage is lectio where one slowly reads the Word, allowing it to sink in. The passage is kept short so a single point may emerge. The second stage is called *meditatio* or meditation and calls forth meaning from what was read. Here you think creatively about the text, using all the senses to bring it alive. The third stage is *oratio*, meaning prayer, and it is where we leave thinking aside and lift our hearts to God. Meditation on the Word inspires this lifting. The fourth and final stage is the stage of *contemplatio* or contemplation, which is the actual resting or abiding in God. Here we have let go of all thoughts and images. We have disposed ourselves simply to be aware of God's presence. Figure 2 shows the interaction and relationship of the parts of *lectio*.

---

[20] Richard Rohr, Adapted from *Silent Compassion: Finding God in Contemplation*, (Cincinnati: Franciscan Media), 63-65.

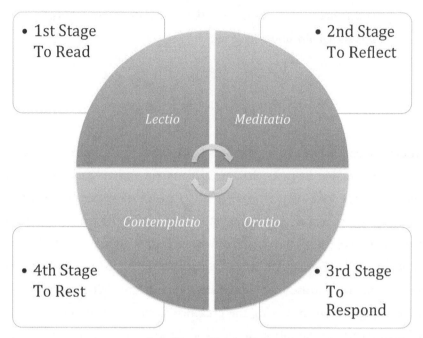

• 1st Stage
  To Read

• 2nd Stage
  To Reflect

Lectio

Meditatio

Contemplatio

Oratio

• 4th Stage
  To Rest

• 3rd Stage
  To
  Respond

Four Stages of Lectio Divina

"Awareness" is the essential element for contemplative prayer, and in our diagram it would be the fourth stage. It is something we still are able to do that creates the possibility for God to break through and for us to experience God as God directly. As we remain aware, we are transformed from within by God's presence as grace. The repetition of this state of prayer will gradually have a profound effect on the manner in which we live, and this transformation will be the test of the authenticity of our prayer, for contemplative prayer and contemplative action, as we shall see, are two sides of the same coin. One caveat needs to be mentioned. These four stages are not fixed steps that are always followed in order. They are more the elements of how *lectio divina* develops. Its movement is towards ever-greater simplicity with the words of Scripture eventually dissolving in presence. Centering Prayer, on the other end of the continuum, simply calls the individual to breathe gently and, when ready, to introduce a sacred word, to focus attention, and then relax into the presence. The phrase that shimmers, a practice that lies midway between *lectio divina* and Centering Prayer, will be the focus of chapter 2.

CONTEMPLATION IN THE EAST AND WEST

It is important to note that in the East, when Buddhists speak of "meditation" and the clearing of the mind of all thought, it is what we in the West mean by "contemplation." Thus, Eastern meditation and Western meditation are very different, since meditation in the West involves creative imagining and thinking. It is often referred to as discursive meditation.[21] Another term frequently used in the East is "mindfulness," which involves paying attention to our thoughts and feelings without analysis or judgment. There is no right or wrong way to feel or think. Mindfulness practice is rooted in Buddhist meditation and has entered the West as a secular practice.

One further note on the experience of presence in both the East and West as it affects our brains: Andrew Newberg and Mark Waldman quote a study of Catholic nuns practicing Centering Prayer and reporting significant neurological changes in their brains as compared to the average brain. And even more noteworthy is the fact that the changes were very much the same as those found in Buddhist monks who came from very different beliefs. Clearly then, practices for clearing the mind of all distractions and thinking, and one then sinking into the present moment with awareness, have more to do with divine presence than they have to do with a common theology or belief system.[22]

---

[21] Discursive meditation is defined as a reasoned application of the mind to some supernatural truth in order to penetrate its meaning, love it, and carry it into practice with the assistance of grace. Aumann, Jordon, *Spiritual Theology, Fourth Ed.* (London: Sheed and Ward, 1986), 319.

[22] Andrew Newberg and Mark Robert Waldman, *How God Changes Your Brain*, (New York: Ballantine Books, 2009), 48.

FURTHER READING

In *Without Buddha I Could Not Be a Christian*, Paul Knitter discusses how Buddhism can help Christians draw on the mystical contents of our faith. He writes,

> *Yes, Buddhism can help Christians be mystical Christians, that is, to enter into divine presence and 'Be one with the Father, to live Christ's life, to be not just a container of the Spirit but an embodiment and expression of the Spirit, to live by and with and in the Spirit, to live and move and have our being in God.'[23]* Knitter continues, *"True, what Christians are after is different than what Buddhists are after. For Christians, it's identification with the Christ-Spirit. For Buddhists, it's realizing their Buddha-nature. And yet, both of these very different experiences have something in common: they are unitive, non-dualistic, mystical experiences in which we find that our own identity is somehow joined with that which is both more than, and at the same time one with, our identity. This is what the Buddhist practices are so good at--achieving such unitive experiences in which the self is so transformed that it finds itself through losing itself.[24]*

[23] Paul F. Knitter, *Without Buddha I Could Not Be a Christian* (London: Oneworld Publications, 2009), 154-155.
[24] Ibid., 155.

2

CONTEMPLATIVE PRAYER

THE POWER OF SIMPLE PRESENCE

As we mentioned in the previous chapter, contemplative prayer can take many forms from the state achieved through *lectio divina* to Centering Prayer. We will be looking at a format somewhere between the two, which we will call *"a phrase that shimmers."*[25] After a consideration of the two tools for this middle path to presence, later in the chapter we will consider other practices that could be employed. The goal or end for which we dispose ourselves is the living Word of God present and communicative. Various spontaneous spiritual experiences give us a sense of what this unitive experience is. It could be the stunning sunset you experienced and the gasp of wonder or the awe and majesty you felt as the giant orange orb slipped beneath the horizon and the heavens became streaked with the many hues of blue and pink. You stop, gaze, and stand for a moment, as if transfixed by the beauty. There is great delight in simply standing and savoring the magnificent spectacle before you. Another may be the holding of a newborn, wiggling and fussing in your strong hands, just gazing into her eyes and adoring her little fingers and beautifully shaped little nails, her rumpled face and the kicking of

---

[25] This is a process and practice taught at The Shalem Institute for Spiritual Formation, Washington, D.C.

her feet. What magic, what wonder! Or it may be the glory of 150 acres of sunflowers bending in the sun as it moves across the noonday sky. Cezanne and the impressionistic school of painting come to mind, as does the abundance of God's gifts to the earth. These are at least three of the many unitive experiences we might have and that same sense of wonder, mystery, and awe await us in any present moment if we are able to dispose ourselves to God's presence and wonder.

Archbishop Rowan Williams, former leader of the Anglican Church, told the Synod of Catholic Bishops in Rome that,

> *Contemplation is very far from being just one kind of thing that Christians do: it is the key to prayer, liturgy, art and ethics, the key to the essence of a renewed humanity that is capable of seeing the world and other subjects in the world with freedom – freedom from self-oriented, acquisitive habits and the distorted understanding that comes from them. To put it boldly, contemplation is the only ultimate answer to the unreal and insane world that our financial systems and our advertising culture and our chaotic and unexamined emotions encourage us to inhabit. To learn contemplative practice is to learn what we need so as to live truthfully and honestly and lovingly. It is a deeply revolutionary matter.*[26]

Such is the importance of what Thomas Merton re-introduced to the Western world in the 1950's and 1960's and his brother Cistercians, William Menninger, Basil Pennington, and Thomas Keating who followed him.

What is contemplative prayer? St. Teresa answers: *"Contemplative prayer – oración mental – in my opinion is nothing else than a close sharing between friends; it means taking time frequently to be alone with him who we*

---

[26] Archbishop Rowan Williams, "The Archbishop of Canterbury's Address," Address to the Synod of Bishops, Rome, October 10, 2012.

know loves us."[27] *Contemplative prayer seeks him 'whom my soul loves.' It is Jesus, and in him, the Father. We seek him, because to desire him is always the beginning of love, and we seek him in that pure faith which causes us to be born of him and to live in him. In this inner prayer we can still meditate, but our attention is fixed on the Lord himself."*[28]

Thinking Versus Awareness

To the testimony of sunsets, newborns and sunflowers, we might add the descriptions of those who have returned from near death experiences. They speak of having partaken of a fuller more abundant life, one devoid of separateness, one of mysterious union with all that had constituted their life. To their voices might be added the seemingly mystical union of lovers in their embrace and passionate love for each other. Suddenly, they lose a sense of separateness and lie in the bliss of union, and the very individuated bodies that got them to this experience become the only inhibitions to total oneness.

We are more than we appear as individuals, and contemplative prayer is one very important path to that sort of union - a union that Thomas Keating has referred to as spiritual awareness. Note his use of the word "awareness" and not "thought." Cynthia Bourgeault describes this kind of awareness as different from the self-reflexive ego, which thinks by means of noting differences and drawing distinctions. For her, *"Spiritual awareness 'thinks' by an innate perception of kinship, of belonging to the whole."*[29] She offers us a clear way of distinguishing the two, thinking versus awareness:

---

[27] *Catechism of the Catholic Church, 2709.*

[28] Ibid.

[29] Cynthia Bourgeault, *Mystical Hope: Trusting in the Mercy of God,* (Boston: Cowley Publications, 2001).

On a bright, sunny day you can set your course on a landfall five miles away from you and sail right to it. But in the fog, you make your way by paying close attention to all the things immediately around you: the deep roll of the sea swells as you enter open ocean, the pungent scent of spruce boughs, or the livelier tempo of the waves as you approach land. You find your way by being sensitively and sensuously connected to exactly where you are, by letting "here" reach out and lead you. You will not learn that in the navigation courses, of course. But it is part of the local knowledge that all the fishermen and natives use to steer by. You know you belong to a place when you can find your way home by feel... If egoic thinking is like sailing by reference to where you are not—by what is out there and up ahead—spiritual awareness is like sailing by reference to where you are. It is a way of 'thinking' at a much more visceral level of yourself-responding to subtle intimations of presence too delicate to pick up at your normal level of awareness, but which emerge like a sea swell from the ground of your being once you relax and allow yourself to belong deeply to the picture.[30]

It is this longing at a level deeper than thinking that draws us to contemplative prayer and is a taste to which we often want to return. Nothing, however, will satisfy as God's very presence, and it is this union for which the longing was planted deep within us from the moment of conception.

Labeling and judging things has a way of keeping us from encountering them in themselves. We get stuck in the labels and judgments without a one-on-one with them as they are, with nothing added. In *The Naked Now*, Richard Rohr speaks of such encountering:

---

[30] Ibid.

Humans tend to think that because they agree or disagree with the idea of a thing, they have realistically encountered the thing itself. Not at all true, says the contemplative. It is necessary to encounter the thing in itself. "Presence" is my word for this encounter, a different way of knowing and touching the moment.[31]

SILENCE, THE GROUND OF BEING

Silence is the bedrock, the foundation stone, the very ground of all existence. It is not only silence that allows us the space to have things that have been simmering to finally come together as an answer or a creative idea, but it is also the origin of deeper relationships, understandings, and identities. Without an appreciation of silence, we are prone to look for the meaning of life in more action, more stimulation, and more possessions in order to lift us out of the boredom and monotony of daily living. Of course, the letdown is inevitable. Fr. Richard Rohr states,

We are in danger of becoming just a shell with less and less inside, and less contact with the depth and reality of things— where all the lasting vitality is found.[32]

New retirees who have not learned to appreciate simply sitting in silence find doing nothing very difficult. Reflection and being still can sometimes be seen as a running from self or from God, from the truths that are within crying out to be heard. Contemplation would have us simply notice an object and gaze at it to let it speak to us. At such times, the simplest of objects, something in nature, a potted plant, a steaming

[31] Richard Rohr, *The Naked Now: Learning to See as the Mystics See*, (Spring Valley: Crossroad Publishing Company) 35, 60, 75.
[32] Richard Rohr, *Letting Go: A Spirituality of Subtraction*, (Cincinnati: Franciscan Media), disc 3.

cup of coffee, or the flame of a burning candle can be a portal taking us from ego-centered considerations to dreams, fantasies, and beyond to a resting in God.

PRACTICE OF THE SILENCE OF THE SENSES

Mother Teresa offers us an excellent portal to contemplation via meditation. She makes clear a way of entering silence where we can access all that is necessary to live quietly and peacefully with openness to the service of others.

To make possible true inner silence, practice:

➢ *Silence of the eyes, by seeking always the beauty and goodness of God everywhere, and closing them to the faults of others and to all that is sinful and disturbing to the soul.*

➢ *Silence of the ears, by listening always to the voice of God and to the cry of the poor and the needy, and closing them to all other voices that come from fallen human nature, such as gossip, tale bearing, and uncharitable words.*

➢ *Silence of the tongue, by praising God and speaking the life-giving Word of God that is the truth, that enlightens and inspires, brings peace, hope, and joy; and by refraining from self-defense and every word that causes darkness, turmoil, pain, and death.*

➢ *Silence of the mind, by opening it to the truth and knowledge of God in prayer and contemplation, like Mary who pondered the marvels of the Lord in her heart, and by closing it to all untruths, distractions, destructive thoughts, rash judgments, false suspicions of others, vengeful thoughts, and desires.*

➢ *Silence of the heart, by loving God with our heart, soul, mind, and strength; loving one another as God loves; and avoiding all selfishness, hatred, envy, jealousy, and greed.*

> ➤ *I shall keep the silence of my heart with greater care, so that in the silence of my heart I hear His words of comfort, and from the fullness of my heart I comfort Jesus in the distressing disguise of the poor. For in the silence and purity of the heart God speaks.*[33]

As mentioned, the above five senses can be an avenue to contemplation. What is sensed can be reduced to a one or two word mantra and be helpful in disposing oneself as an effective tool for contemplation. Let us now turn to the tools for the third form of prayer, contemplation.

THE MODEL: 2 TOOLS, 4 STEPS

We have spoken thus far in this chapter of the power there is in simply being present to God with very little having to be done on our part. The value of silence is absolutely primary in this regard. Let us now take up in detail the concrete way that I would propose to dispose ourselves to God's presence. There are two tools that can assist us in this regard. The first is the tool of breathing, and the second is the use of a phrase or mantra. I like to think of both as incarnational, that is, both have an element of the divine and the human. The breath is something we take for granted, from our first breath in when we take in enough air to utter our first cry until we take our last exhalation and pass to the other side of life. All the breaths between those two constitute our life. So the breath is something that is very natural, life sustaining, and, for the most part, taken for granted.

Yet it also possesses something of the divine. It was God's Spirit that breathed over the waters and brought calm out of chaos. Our breathing can bring us the same calm and tranquility. This pivotal aspect of the breath as divine is something that is shared by each of the Abrahamic religions. Jews hold God's name as sacred and never to be uttered from

---

[33] Mother Teresa, *In the Heart of the World: Thoughts, Stories, and Prayers* (Novato: New World Library, 1997), 17-24.

the diaphragm, the arched back and shoulders expand the rib cage and chest cavity (allowing the lungs to fully expand), and the raising of the chin opens the windpipe to receive the greatest amount of air. So, breathing in and noticing what your body is doing becomes a great instructor.

Breathing out is just as much an instructor as breathing in. We begin by noting that the exhale is very different, and feels very different, from the inhale. It is little work, total relaxing, and exemplified beautifully in the long sigh, which might be considered an aspirated exhalation. What seems to fit quite naturally with the relaxing exhale is an intentional letting go of the muscles of the face. Begin with awareness of the furrowed brow and simply tighten it and then relax it completely. Tighten the eyes and then soften them, tighten the cheeks and relax, clench your teeth then unclench your jaw. Now, to all four actions over the length of an exhalation count of ten: relax the brow, soften the eyes, drop your cheeks, and unclench your jaw. I sometimes imagine the flesh melting off my face or all the tension draining out of my face, through my neck and out my fingers. This is not meant to be a difficult or complex process. Simply think forehead, eyes, cheeks, and jaw. So let us begin with a count of 10 and on the inhalation think: abdomen, shoulder, and chin. Pause for a moment, holding your breath while the oxygen-rich lungs assimilate the enriched air. Then, on the exhalation think forehead, eyes, cheeks, and jaw. Repeat this a total of three times, and you will be completely relaxed. As an aside, this is a wonderful practice to relieve stress in whatever form you may experience it in the course of a day: traffic at a standstill, workload at the office, or upset over what someone said or did. See Appendix B: "Breathing Techniques" for other breathing techniques to achieve different results.

The four steps are then put together in the following way. You begin with a Psalm, scripture passage, or other passage of sacred text no more than a paragraph or two, and read it slowly, listening with the ear of your heart. When you have completed the text, sit quietly and see what words shimmer or speak to your heart. It is out of these shimmering words that you create a mantra, one or two words of not more than a total of four syllables, that can then be set to your pattern of breathing in and breathing out. Thus, for example, your passage may have been taken from Jesus' Last Supper Discourse,[37] and the words that shimmered may have been verse 1: *"Do not let your hearts be troubled. You have faith in God; have faith also in me."* From this phrase you now draw the mantra *"Faith in you"* or *"Heart not troubled"* or *"Faith in God."* It is this mantra that is now synchronized to your breathing in and out. So *"Faith"* as you breathe in, *"in you"* as you gently exhale. This is repeated any number of times until you are comfortable and relaxed with the synchronization. You now begin to let go of the words while you continue awareness of the breathing, then let go of awareness of the breathing and speak to yourself a word of ascent. A word of ascent is simply a word that says you are ready and long for God.

It can be a simple, *"yes."* Speaking your word of ascent, you then simply allow yourself to float gently into God's presence. Continue with simple awareness, looking, noticing, but not engaging in thoughts. It is in this state of awareness that two obstacles to remaining there occur. You will be distracted by voices outside, traffic, the ticking of a clock, the HVAC, or someone's cough. Or you may begin thinking of something you have forgotten to do or needs to be done. You may begin analyzing or questioning, *"Do I have this right?" "I'm not getting it!"* etc. The antidote to distractions and thinking is to return to the mantra synchronized to your breathing as your two tools and repeat the four-step process to redispose yourself to the presence. This process may need to be repeated over and over again. With the 2 tools, 4 steps, and 2 obstacles, we have the process spelled out.

If breathing has both a spiritual and a physical aspect, then so too does a "phrase that shimmers." We are tempted to ask why it "shimmers" in the first place. No doubt it has gotten my attention and touched my heart, addressed a need or interest I may have, or it resonates with me at a deeper level for an unknown reason. From God's side of things, we might say it is a word I was meant to hear, a support or challenge that is

---

[37] John 13:1–17:26

being offered, or an answer to an unspoken prayer. One might look at it as a bit of a personal revelation, as a message meant for me. Yes, divine and physical – might we say incarnational – as is the act of breathing. So we have two tools that have both aspects of reality to them. We use them beginning with their physical side and let God use them with their spiritual side. Both exist within the one praying.

An easy way to picture in a summary fashion where this book hopes to take the reader is to open the palm of your right hand and turn your hand sideways. Now do the same with your left hand so both palms are facing each other. Move your right hand in a horizontal line across to your left palm. There are four incremental steps of the right hand moving toward the left hand. They are comprised of breathing, mantra, letting go, and floating. See Figure #3: *"4-Part Model: Disposing Oneself to the Presence."* The disposing of oneself in order to be in God's presence, represented by the union of the two hands, will meet with two obstacles, namely distractions and thinking. When you are engaged in either – willingly or unwillingly – it would be as if the right hand moves back away from the left and the presence is disrupted.

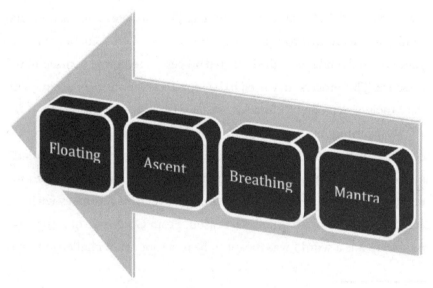

4-Part Model: Disposing Oneself to the Presence

THE MODEL: 2 OBSTACLES

No matter how compelling the unitive experience we may be blessed with, because we are corporeal and human, one or both obstacles are sure to arise and draw us away from the presence. It is natural and it is sure to occur. The first is a simple distraction that draws my attention to something other than awareness; the second is thinking, and it too will do the very same thing. The thinking that removes us from the awareness of contemplation can be as innocent an action of moving from deep gazing into the newborn in my hands to begin thinking, *"How much she looks like her mother!"* The latter thinking of the baby's looks has removed me from the unitive gaze of feasting on the miracle before me in utter awe and amazement. In order to think, I have to become the subject thinking, and the other must become the object thought. So the unity of both is broken, and the joy of simply being in the presence, and one with it, ceases.

Let us take a deeper look at both obstacles and how each could be handled to maintain contemplative awareness. First, there are distractions and there are distractions! A car passing by, the tick of a clock, my heartbeat felt in my temples are minor distractions compared to a screaming child who needs a diaper change, or the incessant coughing of someone in the same room. With the lesser distractions, it is a good idea to make them into white noise. This is something we already do quite naturally. It is why city folks find falling asleep in the country difficult, and country folks find it difficult falling asleep in the city. Each group has accustomed itself to hearing the noise or silence as white noise. We can do the same as we sit in silent prayer. For example, soft talking in another part of the house or hall could be seen as Martha grumbling in the kitchen because she has been left to prepare the dinner. You can imagine yourself to be Mary sitting at the feet of Jesus and gazing into his eyes, paying no attention to the grumbling. Or the humming of the heating or air conditioning could be reinterpreted as the hovering of the Holy Spirit over the group of those praying. Or the ticking of the clock or the throbbing of my heart felt in my temples can be seeing myself as John the Beloved disciple with his head against Jesus' breast hearing his heartbeat. Regarding loud screams or incessant coughing, if you can seek out a quieter place, by all means do so. However, if you must stay put, all you may be able to do is offer the distraction with a prayer such as, *"Lord, I'm here with you for the next 20-30 minutes. Do with me what you will."* One's prayer as distraction becomes an oblation, a loving offering which then gives it some meaning beyond the unavoidable or intrusive noise.

Thinking that takes us out of awareness is a bit more common and a bit more involved. I find I have different kinds of thoughts and different ways of managing each to make them less intrusive. The easiest thoughts to deal with are the simple reminders that surface and on which you dwell, reminders like, *"Don't forget to pick up milk and bread on the way home,"* or *"I forgot to call Jane again!"* If it is important enough to have to remember, simply have a small spiral note pad handy at your prayer table and jot it down. It only takes seconds and leaves your mind free to return to the 2 tools and 4 steps to presence.

A second kind of thought may have to do with something you are working on, and there is a very strong attraction to get the insight down. These engaging thoughts that take you off track and onto another one need simply to be acknowledged and placed aside. It is a very intentional decision you have to make and stick by it. As my spiritual director used to say regarding such insights, if it is important enough, trust that it will come back.

A third kind of thought many have is something that is bothering them and needs their attention, such as an unresolved conflict with a coworker or family member. This thought comes up often in the course of a day and will especially do so now that you are relaxed and open and the issue has an emotional charge to it. For such thoughts I use a bit of mind talk such as, *"This issue will be there after my prayer time"* or Jesus' famous words on worry in Matthew 6:27, 37: *"Can any one of you by worrying add a single hour to your life? ... Seek first the Kingdom..."*

THOMAS KEATING ON "THINKING"

Thomas Keating, the contemporary authority for Centering Prayer, has a very simple four-step plan for disposing oneself to the presence. As already stated above, it is less complex than *lectio divina*. It is comprised of choosing a sacred word and sitting with it comfortably; as silence and calm set it, introduce the sacred word. When you find yourself engaged in thoughts, return gently to the sacred word. With the period ending, remain in silence for a few minutes.[38] In his classic on Centering Prayer, *Open Mind, Open Heart,* Keating lists the five kinds of thinking that keep one from awareness and a direct experience of God's presence. They are:

> ➢ Wanderings of the Imagination
> ➢ Thoughts that Capture the Imagination
> ➢ Psychological Insights into Past Life
> ➢ Analysis of Luminous Darkness
> ➢ Interior Purification[39]

Thoughts as disturbing influences on our ability to simply be aware have been addressed by many spiritual authors and seem to be common to all spiritual traditions. Thomas Keating is the most illustrative and lists the five just mentioned. Knowing them and identifying them for oneself could help in letting them go and keeping them from intruding.

He speaks of the first type as wanderings of the imagination as a boat flowing down the river of consciousness. They may represent past events or present distractions. Rather than looking into the boat to see what is there, the individual simply lets go of any desire to know and returns to the sacred word and to a state of awareness.

---

[38] Thomas Keating, *The Method of Centering Prayer,* (Butler: Contemplative Outreach, Ltd., 2006).

[39] Keating, Thomas, *Open Mind, Open Heart,* (New York: Bloomsbury Academic, 2006), 78ff.

His second uses the boat simile again, but this time the boat captures your attention, motivating you to climb aboard and have a look for yourself. Your sacred word can be very useful in helping you break the spell of captivation.

It is when you have settled into a certain quietness that the third kind of thought can surface. It comes as an insight or the solution to a problem you may be having in a relationship with another person. You may even feel a desire to pray for that person. Such desires should not be responded to and, instead, the sacred word can bring you back into the presence, for this is a time you have set aside for you to listen and for God to have an opportunity to speak. Any temptation to have to think this through because it is so great an insight should be avoided. If it is that important and central to your well being, it will come back again, rest assured.

The fourth kind of thinking surfaces when you are deep in awareness and experiencing a rich and deep satisfaction of God's presence. This experience surfaces in such a way that you begin to look at it and respond to it as a subject to an object. *"Isn't this extraordinary!"* or *"I need to remember how I got here"* are thoughts that bubble to the surface. The very fact you are having them and lingering with them has broken the unitive experience of oneness with God in the presence. When such judgments arise, they need to be placed aside, as you would any other thinking, returning to the sacred word and breathing.

To the fifth and final kind of thinking, Keating devotes an entire chapter.[40] He calls it,

> *Thoughts that represent the unloading of the unconscious and result in an interior purification of prior unresolved experiences."* Regarding this he states: "As the deep peace flowing from centering prayer releases our emotional blocks, insights into the dark side of our personality emerge and

---

[40] Ibid. 95-114.

multiply.... when this dynamism begins to operate in us, our so-called good intentions look like a pile of dirty dishrags. We perceive that we are not as generous as we had believed. This happens because the divine light is shining brighter in our hearts. Divine love, by its very nature, accuses us of our innate selfishness.[41]

Keating, at the minimal end of the contemplative prayer format continuum, begins with simple breathing and then moves to a sacred word. Key to his practice is that the sacred word is the symbol of one's intention to be with God and to live out of that presence. This is basically a two-sides-of-one-coin approach we will be advocating in chapter 3. Thus, the sacred word, not necessarily a holy word such as Jesus or Abba, helps dispose you to the presence. It is made "sacred" by your intention to have it so and might be the simple word "union," "embraced," or "lustrous" as possible examples. After having experienced the presence for 10, 20, or 30 minutes, that same word now serves as an intention "to live out of" the grace that was received. Now fired up, or touched by the experience of presence, one has the eyes, ears, and heart to express that union, embrace, or luster to others.

RICHARD ROHR ON "THINKING"

When the evangelist, Matthew, speaks of the eye being the lamp of the body,[42] he is implying that the I, I am, can view itself from a higher perspective. It is an objectively other place that can view the ego in thought or action. While the ego is not bad, it does have a tendency to take over clouding what you see as yourself.

Beginners in contemplative prayer – and we are all beginners in

---

[41] Ibid. 96.
[42] Matt. 6:22.

some sense – have to work hard at finding this place to stand and from which they can observe themselves. When compulsive thinking is going on, when they cannot rid themselves of distraction, it is very difficult to simply rest in awareness. The observing "I," the I that sees the thinking me will often find itself smiling or filling with tears as it witnesses the compulsive thinking Rohr speaks of to this witness to the self:

> *This knowing of self must be compassionate and calmly objective. It names the moment for what it is, without need to praise or blame my reaction to it.*[43]

ECKHART TOLLE ON "THINKING"

Moving from thinking to awareness is critical for contemplative presence. For Eckhart Tolle, it is a relinquishing of the ego, a giving up everything with which the ego has identified. Speaking of individuals who, through disaster or war, have lost all they have called their own – such as family, possessions, social position, job, physical abilities – are known to have bottomed out and in that very act have found a sacred sense of presence. Tolle likens it to St. Paul's understanding of *"the peace of God which surpasses all understanding."* [44] Tolle states,

> *When there is nothing to identify with anymore, who are you? When forms around you die or death approaches, your sense of Beingness, of I Am, is freed from its entanglement with form. Spirit is released from its imprisonment in matter. You realize your essential identity as formless, as an all-pervasive Presence, of Being prior to all forms, all identification. You realize your true identity as consciousness itself, rather than what consciousness*

---

[43] Richard Rohr, *The Naked Now*, op cit.
[44] Phil. 4:7.

had identified with. That's the peace of God. The ultimate truth
of who you are is not I am this or I am that, but I Am.[45]

Most fundamentally, Tolle would say that you are not your mind, and he develops this idea by explaining thinking and awareness, mind and being. He would hold that being is eternal, ever-present, and is constituted by a single life force that is beyond the many forms of life that are under the mantle of birth and death. But this Being while beyond is very deeply ingrained within every form of physical existence and consequently can be accessed at any moment as one's deepest self or truest nature. This essence can only be experienced when the mind is at rest and one is in a state of awareness. Tolle would say that your attention is fully in the present moment. *As a result, one's being can be experienced, but never understood with one's mind.* To be in such a state is to be in enlightenment. Because being is our very essence, it is immediately accessible to us as the feeling of our own presence. It is the "I am" that is beneath or before the *"I am this"* or *"I am that."*

All of humanity seems saddled with the dreadful affliction of not being able to suspend thinking. As a result, all are suffering from it. Because it is so widespread, it is spoken of and considered normal. In addition to the suffering it causes, it creates a mind-made self that is not grounded in who we really are. In Descartes' famous maxim, *"I think therefore I am,"* he erroneously expressed the basic error of making thinking and being one, as well as making identity equal to thinking. Thus, there is a deeper level of I-ness than my thought. It is the awareness that I am, and in the awareness of the moment, I become both nothing and everything. When you identify with your mind, all the images, past, present, and future can be focused in it as if on a screen, and we begin to live off of the screen, thus blocking or impacting our interactions with others. Is it any wonder we then feel distant or separated from others? Believing that you are your mind is quite disabling and falsely identifies who you are and how you are in relationship to others and with the world.

---

[45] Ekhart Tolle, *A New Earth: Awakening to Your Life's Purpose*, (New York: Penguin Group, 2005).

Tolle speaks of how the beginning of freedom is the realization that you are not the thinker. Once you understand this, you are able to separate yourself from your thinking and observe the thinking in itself. It is in this moment of watching the thinker, that a higher level of consciousness is activated. He outlines the process as follows:

➢ *Pay particular attention to any repetitive thought patterns, those old gramophone records that have been playing in your head perhaps for many years*

➢ *This is what is meant by "watching the thinker." It's another way of saying: listen to the voice in your head, be there as the witnessing presence*

➢ *"There is the voice, and here I am listening to it, watching it"*

➢ *This is I am realization, this sense of your own presence, is not a thought. It arises from beyond the mind*

➢ *So when you listen to a thought, you are aware not only of the thought, but also of yourself as the witness of the thought*

➢ *The thought then loses its power over you and quickly subsides, because you are no longer energizing the mind through identification with it*

➢ *This is the beginning of the end of involuntary and compulsive thinking*

➢ *When a thought subsides, you experience a discontinuity in the mental stream – a gap of "no mind"*

➢ *At first, the gaps will be short, a few seconds perhaps, but gradually they will become longer*

➢ *When these gaps occur, you feel a certain stillness and peace inside you. This is the beginning of your natural state of felt oneness with Being, which is usually obscured by the mind*

➢ *With practice, the sense of stillness and peace will deepen*

➢ *You will also feel a subtle emanation of joy arising from deep within: the joy of Being*[46]

---

[46] Ibid., 33-34.

Think of it as the finger of your right and left hand bound tightly together. See Figure #4: *"Overcoming Intrusive Thinking."* Both hands are torqued and tightly bound as if upset by an intrusive thought.

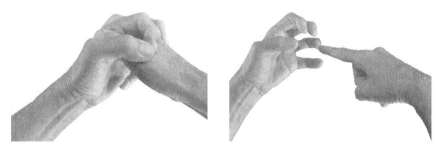

Overcoming Intrusive Thinking

The idea is that the right hand is capable of pulling its fingers away from the left hand and its fingers to observe its turmoil. In doing so, two things become apparent. First, the right is able to witness, as a separate entity, the turmoil of the left hand. This "witness" is a deeper sense of self. It is more soulful and at peace. Second, it is as if the right hand were the power pack for the joint union of hands, and, with it dislodged, the left hand's upset or turmoil begins to wane. It is a relief to realize that inner peace can arise from this sort of witnessing. All it takes is being present and calling forth your witness. It is a surefire way of freeing yourself from your mind.

Tolle speaks of a second approach. In addition to *"watching the thinker,"* you can also create a gap in the mind stream simply by directing the focus of your attention into the now. One does this by becoming intensely conscious of the present moment, which is at the heart of contemplation. The moment may be full attention to my chewing a piece of food, listening to traffic go by, or the formation of a cloud. Being in the now can be part of every moment of everyday life. You practice this by taking any routine activity that normally is only a means to an end and giving it your fullest attention so it becomes an end in itself. Other examples might be each time you walk up and down the stairs at work or home; wash your hands; get in or out of your car; or pay close attention to every step, every movement (even your breathing) and simply be totally present. As you do this, you will experience a deep sense of peace. Let this experienced peace be the measure of success. Tolle counsels, *"Learn to disidentify from your mind. Every time you create a gap in the stream of mind, the light of your consciousness grows stronger."*[47] When you catch yourself smiling, realize that you have come to a point where the content of your mind has lost its power over you, and you are accepting it for what it is. Who you really are does not depend on what you are thinking.

TERESA OF ÁVILA ON "THINKING"

Teresa of Ávila has a wonderful explanation for the four steps she went through to achieve deeper experiences in prayer and moving from thought to awareness to a simple abiding in God. Her metaphor of watering a garden is very popular.[48] The watering can be achieved in one of many ways: by taking water from a well; by getting it from an aqueduct; by drawing it from a stream; or, finally, by having a gentle rain fall from heaven. Each source is a movement deeper in prayer.

In the image of the well, we experience the effort we are making to go to the well to secure the water. It is akin to the Samaritan woman going to the well (John 14) to secure water and where she learns of the living water that Jesus can give her.

With the symbol of the aqueduct, we have the living water from the surrounding countryside reach us as a continuous flow. In such prayer, we have God's consolations in contemplative prayer and know that it is

[47] Ekhart Tolle, *The Power of Now: A Guide to Spiritual Enlightenment*, (Novato: New World Library, 2004).

[48] Sr. Margaret Dorgan, DCM, "St. Teresa of Avila and Water," *Carmelite Nuns of Eldridge Iowa*, http://www.carmelitesofeldridge.org/St.TeresaofAvilaandWater.htm, (October 25, 2015).

not our disposing ourselves, but God's gift of grace. And even though the aqueduct and our prayer may appear dry at times, the flow comes from God's initiative. Water can also come in a stream or small river. Here any efforts of ours are minimal. There is a resting, or abiding in God, with only the maintaining of awareness necessary on our part. In terms of the fruits of such prayer, Teresa lists many of the saints who were formidable in their energies at spreading the Gospel and God's Kingdom in their locales and beyond, whether it be in active apostolates or contemplative lifestyles.

It is "gentle rain" that constitutes the fourth type or level of prayer. Prayer has gone from efforts of disposing ourselves at prayer times in the morning or evening and living out of that presence to seeing God present in the myriad of moments of our day's activities. Both specific prayer times and our moment-to-moment activities are experiences of God's abiding presence. Life is lived in God. This is a very special relationship of friendship with God, as in one where all the secrets of the King are shared with his most intimate attendant and confidant. At times, such a relationship will be experienced as ecstasy, a state involving an experience of mystic self-transcendence.

THE GOD BEYOND THINKING

One might ask why all this focus on not thinking? Who are we at the level that is "deeper-than-thinking"? What is the "it" one encounters in this state of awareness? John Duns Scotus (d. 1308), a Franciscan, and Thomas Aquinas (d. 1274), a Dominican, taught that God is *Being Itself* rather than simply a being out there and an object to be encountered. God is one with all levels of creation. Duns Scotus took the point further teaching the "the univocity of being,"[49] meaning that we can speak with

[49] "Univocity of Being," *Wikipedia*, last modified on February 24, 2015, https://en.wikipedia.org/wiki/Univocity_of_being, (October 25, 2015).

"one voice," consistently and truthfully, about a rock, a tree, an animal, a human, an angel, and God. Aquinas had said that they were the same being only by analogy. It is this "being" as the ground of all existence and our unity with all creation that is encountered at the level of awareness where God manifests God's-self as God is, without the limitations of the words of verbal/vocal prayer or the creative imaginings of meditation. This is a selfless state that takes you beyond what you previously thought of as "your self" to a presence in God. That presence is essentially you and, at the same time, inconceivably greater than you. What a joy it is to experience! St. Paul speaking to the people of Athens hit the nail on the head when he declared: *"From one man he made all the nations, that they should inhabit the whole earth; and he marked out their appointed times in history and the boundaries of their lands. God did this so that they would seek him and perhaps reach out for him and find him, though he is not far from any one of us. 'For in him we live and move and have our being.'"*[50]

When we watch our minds as a witness, we will no doubt find ourselves living in the past or the future. It is the witness that can have the experience of seeing in the now, the present moment, without past or future baggage. Rohr states,

> *Everything that happens to you happens right now; if you can't be present right now, nothing new is ever going to happen to you. You will not experience your experiences; they will not go to any depth in your soul. You really won't grow unless you're willing to live right here, right now—to be present.*[51]

Very often it will take either end of the human emotional continuum – suffering or great joy – to shake us into awareness in the moment and

---

[50] Acts 17:26-28.
[51] Richard Rohr, Adapted from *To Be Awake Is to Live in the Present, Collection of Homilies 2008*, CD, MP3 download, (Albuquerque: Center for Action and Contemplation, 2008

get us out of our head and into our hearts. Having a regular habit of contemplative practice will dispose us to be there regularly. With regularity a habit is born. We will be looking at the formation of a habit of prayer in chapter 5.

THE MONKEY AND THE ELEPHANT

Another way of looking at thinking and contemplation, where the two can work together, is the analogy of the monkey and the elephant. Many involved in meditation tell us that your mind is like a monkey riding an elephant where the monkey represents your conscious thinking mind. The monkey is chattering away and has a multitude of things to say; it never stops and is in a constant frenetic state. On the other hand, the elephant represents your subconscious mind and is carrying the load of all that is going on beneath the surface. It is impossible for the monkey to be able to control the direction in which the elephant is moving, and, truth be told, the elephant is not able to communicate where it wants to go. Our attempts are to silence the chattering monkey or ignore it and have its endless stream of demands and considerations fall on deaf ears. It is what the elephant is trying to tell us that we are listening for and ultimately have both the elephant and the monkey work together so contemplative silence can be achieved.[52]

OVERCOMING DISTRACTION, THINKING, AND DROWSINESS

As we saw earlier in this chapter, there are two tools that are effective in disposing us to be in God's presence, namely breathing and the use of a mantra. We also saw that the four steps to an awareness of God's presence are: mantra, breathing, ascent, and floating. Once there, we remain present

---

[52] Graham Allcott, "Think Productive: Workshops That Work", November 27, 2012, *http//www.thinkproductiveusa.com*.

purely by maintaining awareness. Let it be noted we are doing nothing to coerce God to be present to us. God is always present in love and compassion. Our "work" is to dispose ourselves to maintain awareness. Finally, we considered the two obstacles that will bring us out of the presence, namely distraction and thinking. Let us consider each of them. Thinking is the first. In chapter 1, we looked at the kind of cognitive activity that is peculiar to each form of prayer, and each activity is very different. From verbal/vocal prayer, where we have thinking and speaking, we moved to the deeper level of meditation and the creative act of imaginative thinking. Finally, we moved to the act of pure awareness, where we are completely at the disposal of God's presence. Add to that the fact that one may find it somewhat difficult to remain in simple awareness very long because of distractions or a mind that will not be able to relax and simply be.

When confronting distractions, it is helpful to incorporate them into your awareness. I suggested that the noise made by the air handler of a heating or air conditioning system may be thought of momentarily as the sound of God's Spirit hovering over the room. As another distraction, talking that you overhear from a room nearby or in the corridor may be imagined as the cooking staff working outside the upper room preparing to serve the Last Supper to Jesus and his apostles. In this reimagining, you are there simply sitting next to Jesus and gazing at him. Street traffic outside your prayer space may be seen as the streets of Jerusalem as Jews are gathering to worship in the temple, and finally the ticking of a clock may be the heart of Jesus that John the Evangelist heard as he leaned on Jesus' breast at the Last Supper. The idea is to minimize the distraction and incorporate it into your awareness and let it go, rather than fighting it. Creating white noise – noise that has within it many frequencies of equal intensities – is what city folks do to the distraction of street traffic in trying to sleep. They equalize the frequencies by how they think about the noise. This works in most situations, but there may be a crying child or a neighbor's hacking cough that is very difficult to change our experience of by how we think about it. Another example are the sound machines that are placed outside our counseling offices to drown out conversations to passersby, or they can be used to help one fall asleep.

When the obstacle is compulsive thinking, it is important to remember that you cannot think of two things at the same time, so simply return to an awareness of your breathing and focus on that...and let it go. By that time, the thought you had may no longer have your attention. A second way of dealing with intrusive thinking is to separate yourself from your thinking for a moment and become the one looking at the thinker. It is the "witness" or the "thinker" we saw above. A simple phrase like, *"Just look at him/her carry on! My, my, my"* or a more compassionate response may be, *"Now, now, just relax, let yourself go."* Self-observation helps you dislodge yourself from the compulsive thinking and have a bird's eye view of yourself. The one witnessing is then not at the effect of the thinking, but more at the cause of its cessation. In psychology this is called the self-observing ego. In spirituality we prefer to call it the Witness.

A word needs to be said about drowsiness. Deep breathing, relaxation, and silence can easily induce a sense of drowsiness. The goal in centering ourselves is to be relaxed, yet alert. Key to achieving this is to continuously supply the lungs with a full compliment of oxygen. To achieve this, it is important to keep the chest cavity and the windpipe open. Deep breathing by extending the abdomen and bringing the shoulders back are the elements needed for giving the lungs the full capacity to expand. Lifting the chin, as the abdomen is extended and shoulders are brought back, increases the amount of air that can be inhaled. When you become aware that you are getting drowsy, checking the position of the shoulders and chin become clear indicators that you have diminished the amount of oxygen in your lungs. A simple deep breath by extending the abdomen, drawing back the shoulders, and lifting the chin will bring you back to a state of alertness. Either gently return to repeating your mantra, or if that is not necessary, simply float into awareness. In the practice of Eastern meditation, those meditating sit with their thumbs and index fingers of each hand touching each other. When drowsiness ensues, their fingers will separate naturally and serve as an "alarm clock" and shake them into awareness that they are falling asleep. Either deep breathing or fingers touching can accomplish the same thing.

A final point worth mentioning is that when you find yourself distracted, *awareness* of the distraction is different from *considering* the distraction and having an interior conversation about it. The same is true of thinking. You may suddenly become aware of the fact that you are planning tomorrow's schedule, considering a decision you have to make, or simply entertaining yourself because you have become bored. To reiterate: the two best ways to let go of the distraction or the thinking is either become the Witness to your distraction or thoughts, or return to your mantra and breathing, moving through the four steps to redispose yourself to awareness and the presence. As a last resort, I use a set of noise-cancelling headphones. It creates the perfect space for contemplative prayer.

DISTRACTION AND THINKING? ALL IS NOT LOST!

When noticing distraction or finding yourself engaged in thinking, it is important to realize that all is not lost. Having what is called in the East a "monkey mind" is not an occasion to be dismayed or believe you have failed. Such moments in themselves have a bright side. They are opportunities to redirect yourself, that is, to let go of the distraction or thinking and get back into awareness through breathing and/or use of your mantra. This sort of redirecting is akin to building a mental muscle. This redirecting is the same skill you would employ if distracted at work or in a conversation with a family member. Exercising the mental muscle brings you back to the task you really need to be doing rather than giving in to and engaging in the distraction. In your workplace or around the house, it can keep you from idly engaging in diversionary tactics such as checking emails, responding to popup ads, or answering a question on Google that has no relationship to what you are doing. Exercising it can also keep you from finishing off the half-gallon of ice cream in the freezer or the box of chocolates on the sideboard. Yes, the first step is noticing that you are distracted or thinking of other things – all diversionary in nature. Noticing what your mind is absorbed in and gently bringing your attention back to your breath and mantra is flexing and strengthening your willpower muscle. Studies confirm that such daily centering can help your prefrontal cortex – the brain's command center – grow as well as shrinking the amygdala – the impulse center of the brain – in the short time of two months.[53] Such centering changes the connection between these two areas. *"The connection between the amygdala and the rest of the brain gets weaker, while the connections between areas associated with attention and concentration get stronger."*[54]

WRESTLING WITH DEMONS

Often on contemplative retreats, individuals will ask whether such desirable states of awareness, where we let go completely, might not allow space for the forces of evil to enter our consciousness. It is an honest concern. It is important to note that when letting go of thoughts and distractions and fostering awareness, we are never losing our free will. That is, unlike hypnotism, we are always able to return to thinking, and thus move from awareness to decision making. Contemplative presence is not to be confused with the heresy of Quietism.[55] Entering fully into

---

[53] Tom Ireland, "What Does Mindfulness Meditation Do to Your Brain," *Scientific American*, last modified June 12, 2014, *http://blogs.scientificamerican.com/guest-blog/what-does-mindfulness-meditation-do-to-your-brain/*, (October 26, 2015)

[54] Ibid.

[55] Merriam Webster, s.v. "Quietism," accessed October 25, 2015, *http://www.merriam-webster.com*, A system of religious mysticism that taught the perfection and spiritual peace can be attained by the annihilation of the will and passive absorption in contemplation of God. It was condemned by the Catholic Church. (October 26, 2015).

the silence of one's heart nevertheless can be unnerving. Whether it was Moses or Jesus, facing oneself can arouse both "demons" and "angels," and for us it can also be a confrontation of our past failures or future fears. The Gospel of Mark states, *"And he was in the wilderness forty days, being tempted by Satan. He was with the wild animals, and angels attended him."*[56] And it can, more importantly, be a time of great union affording you space and insight. In the present moment, we can encounter all we need for the moment, and putting all thoughts and distractions aside, the present moment can offer us a sense of relief and renewal. True, retreating to the monastery or to the desert within and encountering silence can be a bit unnerving, and it is important to know we are safe from evil forces, for our will can never be compromised, and in the awareness of the moment we can find safety.

"It's Not the Hand You're Dealt but How You Play It"

Clearly life for most folks is not easy, nor is it ever fair. It has been said that those who are successful have learned how to play the hand they have been dealt. In the analogy, the cards can keep us from breaking through into the present moment. Our emotions have a way of not always being as helpful as they can be at times when we look at the hand we have been dealt. In any given situation, we need to acknowledge and honor what we are feeling, and it is also helpful to recognize that what is occurring outside of ourselves and our emotions is neither, in itself, positive nor negative, that all occurrences are basically neutral. It is what we add to the occurrence that creates the feeling of an emotion regarding it. For example, we can take the occurrence "rainy day." What comes up for you when awakening is that you see it is raining, and you have to prepare for a big meeting that morning. Are you feeling positive, neutral,

---

[56] Mark 1:13.

or negative? Consider, if you will, that "rainy day" is neutral in itself; it is not positive or negative. Most often you will find that the positive or negative balance that you add to it to create your feelings about it have to do with past experiences of rainy days in general. For example, for me as a child, a rainy day was not so much a downer in that we could not go out to play, but an upper in that mom would play with us indoors. We would play restaurant, grocery store, Arabs in their desert with tents created with poles, broom handles and blankets, or we would work in our rainy-day activity books. Who would not look forward to such days? As an adult, therefore, fond memories and realigning what I will wear to weather the storm are all part of a very positive experience. It should be remembered that even if there are not positive experiences to add to the occurrence, it does not mean you cannot recreate the emotion by seeing the good in what has befallen you. It is true that every cloud does have a silver lining; you have to search for it. Do this often enough, and you will begin to create your own positive experiences. I am reminded of the daily occurrence of someone following me too closely on the one-lane country roads where I live. I know all the slow down lanes along routes from my home to the city where I can slow down, pull over, and wave them to pass, saying to myself as I smile them by, *"After you, sir/ma'am, you probably need to get there sooner than I do. Be my guest."* It needs to be acknowledged that it is very difficult to think of disasters, tragedies, and acts of violence, as "neutral," and that they are evil in themselves must be stated as such. What must also be said, however, is that the victims or objects of such events will often acknowledge that there was a presence of the divine, or that in some way there was a blessing that came of such and such an event. This very statement is adding a positive value to the act.

OTHER PRACTICES

THE PRACTICE OF MINDFULNESS

Being in the moment, aware of what I'm doing brings life and luster to even the most mundane of things like washing dishes. While a sink full of dirty dishes may be the last thing you would want to tackle as a way of relaxing, studies have found that it can be incredibly relaxing. In a study at Florida State University, student and faculty researchers found that mindfully washing dishes actually calms the mind and can reduce stress appreciably. As a study in the journal *Mindfulness*,[57] it sought whether washing dishes could serve as a contemplative practice and foster calm and presence. Researchers found that mindful dishwashers who smelled the dishwashing liquid, as well as felt the warmth of the water, the comfort of the suds, and the manipulation of the dishes and washcloth reported a decrease in nervousness by 27% with an increase in mental inspiration of 25%. The control group reported no benefits. The same exercise of awareness can be done with slowly, thoughtfully eating a single raisin or blueberry.

Everything we see in our world can be a practice or portal for contemplative prayer. It can be an object that attracts your attention naturally, like a sunset or special song, a work of art or a photo of a loved one. It can also be something rather commonplace like a tree swaying in the wind or the hum of the refrigerator. All it takes is to pay attention, to sit quietly and allow the object to be itself. The image, coupled with some deep breathing, creates the moment for a deeper awareness of the ground of being to the mystery that lies beneath all the manifestations of creation. One is reminded of the words of St. Paul in the Epistle to the Colossians: *"For in him were created all things in heaven and on earth,*

---

[57] Alexandra Sifferlin, "Washing Dishes Is a Really Great Stress Reliever, Science Says," September 20, 2015, *MNT*, http://www.medicalnewstoday.com, November 6, 2015.

the visible and the invisible, whether thrones or dominions or principalities or powers; all things were created through him and for him. He is before all things, and in him all things hold together.[58]

In the words of Franciscan Sister and scientist Ilia Delio,

> *Christ is the purpose of this universe, and as exemplar of creation, [Christ is] the model of what is intended for this universe, that is, union and transformation in God....Because the universe has a 'plan,' we can speak of the evolution of this plan as the unfolding of Christ in the universe, who is 'the mystery hidden from the beginning.'*[59]

Teilhard de Chardin, the French paleontologist, writes:

> *I am not speaking metaphorically when I say that it is throughout the length and breadth and depth of the world in movement that man [sic] can attain the experience and vision of his God.*[60] In another place he says, *"By means of all created things, without exception, the divine assails us, penetrates us, and molds us. We imagined [the divine] as distant and inaccessible, when in fact we live steeped in its burning layers.*[61]

Whatever stops and moves us, whatever is before our eyes, whatever we enjoy at one level, like the first morning cup of warm brew, all become practices or portals for contemplative presence. Nothing is profane; all is sacred. It is by God's grace that in disposing ourselves to the present

---

[58] Col. 1:15-17.

[59] Eph. 3:9.

[60] Ilia Delio, O.S.F., *Christ In Evolution*, (New York: Orbis Books, 2008), 8-9.

[61] Pierre Teilhard de Chardin, *The Divine Milieu*, (New York: William Collins Sons & Co., 1960), 36.

moment we come to see and honor the connection that binds our deepest longings inextricably to the face of God.

As we become more sensitized to the ordinary becoming extraordinary just by our noticing, simple things take on a new luster and become moments of deep joy. Among them might be included:

➢ First cup of morning coffee
➢ Sun on my face
➢ Beginning the third quarter mile of a run
➢ Sun rising through the trees
➢ Sun setting casting golden rays over a landscape
➢ Flowerbeds of ground cover
➢ Fields of grazing cows
➢ Lying on a freshly cut lawn
➢ Horses swiping each other with their tails as a way of keeping flies at bay
➢ Surprise spring house on an old farm
➢ Smell of garlic and onion browning in a skillet
➢ Fragrant lilac or lavender candle burning
➢ V-formation of birds on the wing
➢ Newly planted corn fields
➢ Bouquets of sunflowers
➢ Seeing an Amish horse and buggy on a country road
➢ Sound of cicadas
➢ Glow of fireflies

THE PRACTICE OF THE SACRAMENT OF THE PRESENT MOMENT

Anyone can enter a journey into the spiritual life according to Jean-Pierre de Caussade (1675-1751). A French Jesuit and chaplain to a cloistered order of religious nuns in Nancy, France, de Caussade taught them that it takes no special talent, only a longing to know God and to be in union with him. He believed that God speaks to every person through what happens to them moment by moment, and the only real duty we have is to keep one's gaze fixed on the Lord and constantly listening so as to hear, understand, and immediately obey his will. The only condition necessary for such a state of self-surrender is the present moment in which the soul, as he would say, *"Light as a feather, fluid as water, innocent as a child, responds to every movement of grace like a floating balloon."*[62] The individual was counseled not to look for the holiness *of* things, but the holiness *in* things and abandonment was as the heart of his teaching. Caussade's key theme is:

> *If we have abandoned ourselves to God, there is only one rule for us: the duty of the present moment."* Beevers explains that Caussade is insisting, *"Over and over again, that we must live from minute to minute. The past is past, the future is yet to be. There is nothing we can do about either, but we can deal with what is happening moment by moment."*[63] Living in the present is Presence of its very nature. True mystics according to Beevers, *"are more practical than most people. They seek reality; we too often are satisfied with the ephemeral. They want God as he is; we want God as we imagine him to be.*[64]

The Practice of "Om"

The great religions of the world that seek union with God through prayer have pointed out ways to achieve that union. As the Catholic Church

---

[62] Jean-Pierre de Caussade, "Jean-Pierre de Caussade Quotes," *AZ Quotes*, http://www.azquotes.com/quote/747547, (January 3, 2016).

[63] John Beevers, trans., *Abandonment to Divine Providence by Jean-Pierre de Caussade*, (New York: Doubleday Religious Publishing Group: 1975), 20.

[64] Ibid., 21.

rejects nothing of what is true in these religions, the Congregation for the Doctrine of the Faith has stated that, *"Neither should these ways be rejected out of hand simply because they are not Christian. On the contrary, one can take from them what is useful so long as the Christian conception of prayer, its logic and requirements are never obscured."* [65] It is within this spirit of openness that some Eastern practices can enrich our own contemplative tradition.

Chanting is a time-honored practice both in East and the West, which in a very natural way draws our focus to the present and calms the mind. The act of breathing and forming sounds has a way of bringing body and mind together. There are as many ways to chant as there are individuals with different lungs, throats, and vocal cords. Exploring different kinds of chant or creating your own chant are ways to move you from head to heart, from thinking to awareness, from ego to other. Perhaps the most familiar chant is *"Om."* The Hindu tradition holds that Om is the original and foundational vibration of the created world and, therefore, the sound that holds all other sounds. In Sanskrit it is called pranava, which means that it fills all of life as well as our prana, breath. Thus, *"Om"* represents the fullness of all that is and encompasses all things. It has no beginning and no end. One exercise is to chant this single syllable slowly for five minutes or more and end it with a period of silence. Sit tall; breathe deeply. As you exhale, vocalize the three sounds of Om, A-U-M, on a single tone. As you do so, feel the sound moving up and outward in your breath. Beginning in your abdomen – aah – moving to your chest cavity – ooh – vibrating in your lips and nasal passages – mm. Repeat it a second time along with a deep breath, and chant *"Om"* again, slowly shaping the vowels and closing your mouth to a hum. Repeat as many times as feels right for you, all the while letting all other thoughts and sensations disappear. When distracted or you begin thinking, simply return your focus to breath and sound and the way it feels in your body. When the time is right for you, just let the chant gently subside into a deep silence.

[65] Letter to the Bishops of the Catholic Church on Some Aspects of Christian Meditation, Congregation for the Doctive of the Faith, V. Questions of Method, 16.

Remain there for five to 10 minutes. Reflect for a moment on what the experience was like and how would you describe it.

THE PRACTICE OF "WALKING MEDITATION"

Thích Nhất Hạnh, a renowned Vietnamese Buddhist monk, teacher, author, poet, and peace activist, recommends that you take short steps in complete relaxation, walking with a smile on your lips and your heart open to an experience of peace. Make your steps those of a healthy and secure person. Feel all the worries and concerns drop from you as you walk. Learning to walk like this will give you great peace and anyone can do it.[66]

AFTER SCRIPTURE, A SPECIAL PLACE FOR POETRY

Next to a scriptural phrase that shimmers, poetry holds a special place of honor as a practice to dispose oneself to the divine presence. Like a scriptural mantra, it is verbal and very easily synchronized to breathing in and breathing out. Because of its use of metaphors and other figures of speech, it can go directly to our inner experience. Mirabai Starr has stated that, *"Poetry is a gateway into unitive consciousness. It knocks on the doors of the heart and the heart opens. Poets speak truth in a very naked way that bypasses the rational mind. Poetry evokes, rather than describes."* [67] The power of poetry is its ability to connect us to our True Self, pressing through our ego's need for self-defense and justification. Good poetry opens us

---

[66] Thich Nhat Hanh, "A Guide to Walking Meditation," *Dhamma Talks,* last updated January 14, 2016, *http://www.dhammatalks.net/Books2/Thich_Nhat_Hanh_A_Guide_to_Walking_Meditation.htm* (October 26, 2015).

[67] Richard Rohr and Mirabai Starr, "Unitive Consciousness: An Eastern Perspective," an unpublished webcast, Center for Action and Contemplation, Albuquerque, NM, August 18, 2015.

directly to experience. Kabir, a 15th century religious reformer, was an artist and musician. His metaphor for unitive consciousness remains fresh and illustrative: *"All know that the drop merges into the ocean, but few know that the ocean merges into the drop."*[68]

Poetry creates the leap from mind to heart and direct experience. It does this by the use of metaphor. Religious language must speak in metaphors because it points to the ineffable, what is beyond words, yet what can be experienced. The Mystery, once you experience it, you will know it in the fullest sense that a human being is able to know. Merton is credited to have said that in hearing the words of Jesus of the necessity *"to eat my flesh and drink my blood,"* the hearer/believer is supposed to stop breathing for a while. Instead we enter into theological debate. Metaphor comes from the Greek meaning, *"to carry across"* as in to carry the reader across to the level of experience. Left brain folks await the perfect definition. Right brain folks realize it is better to describe through the use of metaphor and indirectly, for the metaphor is the finger that points to the moon and not the moon itself. As Emily Dickinson would have it,

> *"Tell all the truth but tell it slant*
> *The Truth must dazzle gradually*
> *Or every man be blind --."* [69]

One would think there is a fine line between scripture and poetry perhaps because much of scripture is poetry and vice versa. Poetry fits nicely under verbal/vocal as a prayer type. Much of poetry, like scripture, can be creative, imaginative, and inspired. Its rich imagery calls forth

---

[68] Daniel Ladinsky, *Love Poems from God: Twelve Sacred Voices from the East and West*, (New York: Penguin Compass, 2002), 209.
[69] Emily Dickinson, "Tell all the truth but tell it slant," *The Poems of Emily Dickinson: Reading Edition* edited by Ralph W. Franklin, (Cambridge: The Belknap Press of Harvard University Press: 1998).

the divine within the ordinary and places it squarely before the mind for consideration. The well is deep and filled with living water, especially in the poetry of such mystics as John of the Cross and Teresa of Ávila. Of John of the Cross' *"The Spiritual Canticle,"* James Finley would have us look not just at its subject matter. Instead, he writes, *"We are to read it as the opening up of our hearts, that we might rest in…this oneness and communion in each other and as each other. In your most childlike hour, you're asked to surrender to that oneness. And a transformative experience occurs. Love is transforming us into itself."*[70]

John of the Cross

Let us look at several poetic examples that can open our hearts through the use of analogy, metaphor, or simile so they might rest in God. The following poem of John of the Cross is a conversation between lovers and is similar to that found in *The Song of Songs* in the Old Testament:

Bride
In the inner wine cellar
I drank of my beloved, and when I went abroad
Through all this valley
I no longer knew anything,
And lost the herd that I was following.

There he gave me his breast;
There he taught me a sweet and living knowledge;
And I gave myself to him,
Keeping nothing back;
There I promised to be his bride.

[70] Richard Rohr and James Finley, *Intimacy: The Divine Ambush* MP3, (Albuquerque: Center for Action and Contemplation, 2013).

Now I occupy my soul
And all my energy in his service;
I no longer tend the herd,
Nor have I any other work
Now that my every act is love

With flowers and emeralds
Chosen on cool mornings
We shall weave garlands
Flowering in your love,
And bound with one hair of mine.

You considered
That one hair fluttering at my neck;
You gazed at it upon my neck;
And it captivated you;
And one of my eyes wounded you.

When you looked at me
Your eyes imprinted your grace in me;
For this you loved me ardently;
And thus my eyes deserved
To adore what they beheld in you.

Do not despise me;
For if, before, you found me dark,
Now truly you can look at me
Since you have looked
And left in me grace and beauty.

Bridegroom

The small white dove
Has returned to the ark with an olive branch;
And now the turtledove
Has found its longed-for mate
By the green river banks.

She lived in solitude,
And now in solitude has built her nest;
And in solitude he guides her,
He alone, who also bears
In solitude the wound of love.[71]

Let the poem serve as the passage from scripture served. Perhaps the phrase that shimmered was *"I drank of my beloved,"* the mantra *"I drank."* The latter, synchronized to breathing, becomes the tool for disposing oneself to the presence.

MARY OLIVER

A contemporary poet, Mary Oliver, can look at a swan taking flight and make a connection with the divine presence:

The Swan – Mary Oliver

Did you too see it, drifting, all night, on the black river?
Did you see it in the morning, rising into the silvery air -
An armful of white blossoms,

....

---

[71] John of the Cross, "Bride," *John of the Cross: Selected Writings* edited by Kieran Kavanaugh, O.C.D., (Mahwah: Paulist Press, 1987), 225-226.

And did you feel it, in your heart, how it pertained to everything?

And have you too finally figured out what beauty is for?
And have you changed your life?[72]

In this poetic example, what may come to mind is the image of a white cross in motion and your mantra, rather than one or two words, might be the cross moving forward with every breath in and every breath out, in out, in out, eventually allowing the image to fade, since it is a thought, and continuing with letting go of awareness of breathing to floating into God's presence. Mantras or images for synchronization to breathing are rich and varied.

RAINER MARIA RILKE

Extinguish Thou My Eyes by Rilke, is for me, the answer of my indefatigable desire for union with God, no matter what in life assails me.

Extinguish Thou My Eyes

Extinguish Thou my eyes: I still can see Thee,
Deprive my ears of sound: I still can hear Thee,
And without feet I still can come to Thee,
And without voice I still can call to Thee.
Sever my arms from me, I still will hold Thee
....
Arrest my heart, my brain will keep on beating,

---

[72] Mary Oliver, "The Swan," *Swan: Poems and Prose Poems*, (Boston: Beacon Press, 2010).

And should Thy fire at last my brain consume,
The flowing of my blood will carry Thee.[73]

Thomas Ryan

Finally, an especially poignant poem I have used before the Blessed Sacrament is "Benediction" by Paulist Father Tom Ryan. It has him experiencing a moonlit night as being before the Blessed Sacrament in a church.

Benediction

Sitting at the end of the dock
my first night on the island,
full moon shining like
an elevated host held by
the fingertips of the mountain
with its burley shoulders wrapped
in a dark forest-green cape.

Crickets chant in soft, adoring chorus
and beavers swim by my feet
slapping their tails in acclamation
as tufts of cloud-like incense float by
before the monstrance of the moon glow
with tree tops bowing their heads

in the Spirit-breath
of the late night breeze

---

[73] Rainer Maria Rilke, "Extinguish Thou My Eyes," last modified January 13, 2013, http://www.poemhunter.com/poem/extinguish-thou-my-eyes/, (November 2, 2015).

while the stars above
glow like benediction candles
over le Lac du Saint Sacrament.[74]

How easy it is to move from nature to poetic expression!

ANIMA CHRISTI

Two prayers that have been part of my contemplative practice over the years have been the *Anima Christi* and *The Suscipe* of St. Ignatius.

The Anima Christi

Soul of Christ, sanctify me.
Body of Christ, sanctify me.
Blood of Christ, inebriate me.
Water from the side of Christ, wash me.
Passion of Christ, strengthen me.
O Good Jesus, hear me.
Within Thy wounds hide me.
Suffer me not to be separated from thee.
From the malignant enemy defend me.
In the hour of my death call me.
And bid me come unto Thee,
That with all They saints,
I may praise thee
Forever and ever.
Amen.

---

[74] Thomas Ryan, CSP, "Benediction," *Benediction: Beauty and Contemplative Poetry, Living Contemplatively*, last modified September 27, 2013, http://www. livingcontemplatively.org, (October 30, 2015).

For a possible mantra, I chose, *"Sanctify and inebriate me."*

SUSCIPE

The Suscipe of St. Ignatius is a resignation and a complete submission to God.

> *The Suscipe*
>
> *Take, Lord, receive all my liberty,*
> *my memory, my understanding, and my entire will*
> *-- all that I have and call my own.*
> *You have given all to me.*
> *To you, O Lord, I return it.*
> *Everything is yours, do with it what you will.*
> *Give me only your love and your grace.*
> *That is enough for me.*[75]

"Only your love and grace" was the mantra chosen.

TEILHARD DE CHARDIN

A third and final example of a prayer that for me moves easily into contemplation is Teilhard de Chardin's reflection on aging.

> *When the signs of age begin to mark my body (and still more*
> *when they touch my mind); when the ill that is to diminish me*
> *or carry me off strikes from without or is born within me; when*

---

[75] St. Ignatius of Loyola, "Suscipe," *Ignatian Prayers,* last updated September 27, 2014, http://www.Catholic-Resources.org, (October 30, 2015).

the painful moment comes in which I suddenly awaken to the fact I am losing hold of myself and am absolutely passive within the hands of the great, unknown forces that have formed me in all those dark moments, O God, grant that I may understand that it is you who are painfully parting the fibers of my being in order to penetrate to the very marrow of my substance and bear me away within yourself.

An easy mantra might be "Yes, Lord" or "Bear me away."

Haikus

Let the following serve as an example:

> *There is the old pond!*
> *Lo, into it jumps a frog:*
> *hark, water's music!*
> *(Translated by John Bryan)*

> *The silent old pond*
> *a mirror of ancient calm,*
> *a frog-leaps-in splash.*
> *(Translated by Dion O'Donnol)*

Some who seek a more creative practice have found the writing of a haiku very helpful. A haiku is a Japanese poetic form of 17 syllables, in three lines of five, seven, and five. Haikus traditionally evoke images from the world of nature. Appendix C: *"How to Write a Haiku"* offers a brief lesson on how to write a haiku.

MOVING FROM ONE PRAYER TYPE TO ANOTHER

Initially, we began with using only one type of practice, that of a scripture passage or a verse of a psalm, and extracting from that reading a phrase that shimmers and reducing it to a two-word mantra. The idea is to move from a point that involves thinking to a minimal focus, which is easy to let go of and move to simple awareness. There are a myriad of different practices, all of which accomplish the same end – a disposal of the self to awareness and, thus, to encounter God. We then looked at poetry and several prayers as tools to achieve this same disposing of ourselves. A song or hymn, a paragraph from a spiritual source, a work of art or an object in nature – all also can serve to focus our attention and, once synchronized to breathing, either as a word or image, can be let go, enabling us to enter a state of awareness. The third and fourth steps of ascent and floating move the subject as one who is disposed to one who is in the presence. After many years of praying this way, I have found that very little is needed, not only to begin specified times of contemplative prayer, but to steal five or ten minutes in the course of a day. Phrases I use most often are, *"Come Lord (inhale) Je-sus (exhale)"* or *"Here I (inhale) am Lord (exhale)."*

St. Teresa of Ávila was very quick to advise her sisters to *"Pray as you can, not as you ought."* This dictum is especially true in the area of contemplative prayer. Anything that touches your heart, anything that takes you deeper, anything that puts you in a state of recollection can serve as a pathway or a portal to communion with God. Thus, there are situations, events, things in your daily routine that stir and move you inward. Note these, cultivate these, notice what it is about them that appeal to you. So the scent of a candle, the warmth of the sun on your face, the multitude of shades of green as the evening sun filters through the leaves of a tree, the recall of a childhood memory, tasting a single plump fresh blackberry, a gentle breeze on a summer's day – all portals to presence and all mirror in varying degrees the image of the Creator.

We have focused on a word or two that surface from a scripture passage or a word or image from a poem or prayer, yet the source of a mantra could be a work of art, a mystery of the rosary, a song, or a gesture. I am reminded of the popular song, *Spirit of the Living God*, or *Open My Ears, Lord* and how gesture and song can give rise to a sacred word or two in order to dispose me to the presence. Try singing the words, *"Spirit of the living God, fall afresh on me"* and as you do, gently reach out to God with both your hands, feeling the longing you have for God. Draw your hands to your face, turning your palms and gently bringing them down over your face, as if the oil of gladness spoken of in the scriptures was washing over you. Repeat it as you sing the line again. Then as you sing, *"Melt me, mold me, fill me, use me"* make gestures of wiggling your fingers with palms up for a flame, then a shapely vase for *"mold me,"* then palms rising as if in a vase for *"fill me,"* and finally, palms moving out away from you for *"use me."* Then repeat the opening line along with the hand gestures. As you sign the song, let your movements speak to you of your deepest longing for God's grace and choose what it is you long for most, being melted, molded, filled or used by your loving God, and make the words *"melt me," "mold me," "fill me,"* or *"use me"* your mantra for prayer. Letting go of the words, awareness of the breathing, and floating into God's presence will then dispose you for God's grace, specifically in terms of your deepest longing to be transformed. How often we will be surprised at the gift of transforming union! Scripture, Psalms, Icons, poems, adoration before the Blessed Sacrament enthroned in a monstrance, a mystery of the rosary, a drawing or other artwork you have created, all serve as a marvelous gateway to presence. It is all about what touches your heart, so you are able to move from head to heart into the affective domain.

Some find it helpful to use the three readings of the coming Sunday's Mass on Monday, Wednesday and Friday respectively, and from each of them to draw a phrase that shimmers for sitting in the silence. The experience of such contemplative moments becomes a prayerful preparation for worship the following Sunday. In chapter 3, we shall develop a way of creating lived experiences out of such texts. Using the Sunday readings as a basis for contemplative prayer creates a wonderful opportunity to hear how the priest or deacon's homily supports your prayer life or how it challenges you still further. If we preachers had the great gift of such feedback from our people, it would enhance our preaching. It is surprising how 10 to 20 minutes of such contemplative prayer can have a rippling effect in both our lives and the lives of those with whom we come in contact.

Let us look creatively at possible changes in prayer routines and moving among the three columns or types of prayer, as detailed in chapter 1. So, for example, if you already pray the Liturgy of the Hours, try stopping when a phrase of an antiphon or psalm shimmers (Verbal/Vocal Prayer) and move to column two (Meditation) then three (Contemplation), or go to three directly. The same can be done with the rosary and mentioning any of the individual mysteries, such as Joyful, Sorrowful, Glorious, or Luminous. In such cases, praying the rosary may begin as verbal/vocal prayer with the Hail Mary's, may move to meditation at the stating of one of the mysteries, and end up as contemplative. In these ways of moving from one type of prayer to the other, contemplative presence becomes less textbook and more freewheeling.

A final practice may be the simplest of all. It may be the simple presence that is achieved by gazing at the flame of a scented candle – lavender is a very soothing choice – and taking in its flickering and scent or listening to the gong of a singing bowl and following the sound as it loses itself in you.

An interesting question arises: Which of the three types of prayer (Verbal/Vocal, Meditation, or Contemplation) am I most comfortable using? Which do I use most often? Which do I find most transformative? The caution involved in using verbal/vocal exclusively has to do with the criticism Jesus had of the Pharisees' use of it. They became more concerned with the reciting of prayers and the keeping of holy days, but their hearts were far from caring for others.[76] Thus, the danger comes in feeling good or satisfied from simply performing the work and has little or nothing to do with choices animated or graced by those prayers. Of course, that is not to say that verbal/vocal prayer does not have a place in one's prayer life. It is just to admit the caution as the saying goes that, *"A bad kiss is worse than no kiss."* Meditation does allow for a deeper personal engagement in the story, parable, or Psalm that is being used to draw us deeper into an understanding of our own thoughts and feelings. However, when it comes to abandoning oneself before God and allowing God to take over, contemplation, where thought is eschewed and awareness fostered, is to place ourselves within the reach of a *"jealous God"* who wants us heart and soul! Disposing ourselves to be there now and having a way of creating intentions out of that graced presence, the latter of which will be the subject of our next chapter, can make all the difference in the world. After some time at a renewed prayer life, it could be advantageous to see what percentages of your days at prayer are committed to each type. Having done that for myself, contemplative presence clearly is the frontrunner, with verbal/vocal in second place. Noting percentages and benefits received from each, you are then prepared to increase whichever type of prayer you might like to see improved.

The preceding methods have been offered as a variety of approaches, all with the same intent, to pray as you are most able to, not as others have prescribed for you. In short, find your practice and practice it. Find your wisdom figure and follow him/her. Find your spiritual community and be faithful to it. This is important if you are not to float around without any accountability for what you may too easily conjure in your own solitary mind. It is not healthy to have your ego being both the decider and chooser in any given moment.

---

[76] Mark 2:3-28.

CHAPTER

3

CONTEMPLATIVE ACTION

MOVING FROM CONTEMPLATIVE PRAYER TO CONTEMPLATIVE ACTION

Moving from contemplative prayer to contemplative action is at the very heart of the matter. It is the motivation driving the writing of this book. What is the key to understanding the grace of being in God's presence and having that grace transform the individual in ways that make a difference, in ways that others see a change? I had only been accustomed to praying for something in particular, e.g., the healing of a friend or the offer of a new job - that sort of thing. It was through the use of verbal/vocal prayer and a specific intention that was at the heart of such prayer. Meditation, as the second form of prayer, did not seem to gear itself to petitions of this kind. But contemplative prayer was a different matter. If one could use a sacred word or words as a way of disposing oneself to the presence of a God who is acting and present at all times, and if those words are representative of one's need for healing, could not God's presence and one's awareness of that presence serve as a healing balm, an "answer" to prayer? The answer, of course, would not be verbal or conceptual, but more an experience of the divine, a coming to peace with the need that was presented. It would be akin to sitting across from a friend at dinner, completely immersed in each other's presence and not asking for anything in particular, but being assured that he or she was with you 100% in whatever struggle or challenge you were facing. It would be the relationship and the presence that would be the answer, even before a word or request was upon your lips.

Sitting in the silence and disposing oneself to be aware without thinking contributes to an experience of peace and tranquility. At the very least, and these are no small rewards of grace, you will feel grateful for the present moment that was experienced; you will feel a sense of greater generosity towards others, and you will feel as if guided in what to do next. This fertile ground becomes the seedbed for any number of intentions you may wish to make. So, out of a sense of gratitude, might come the intention now to greet an individual you have paid little attention to in this way. This would be called a specific intention. Out of a sense of generosity, you might intend to look at the cash in your wallet and put half in the poor box at church on Sunday. This would be called a general intention of helping those in need. Finally, out of a feeling of being guided, you might make an attitudinal intention to move about the day responding to God's Spirit as it moves you. For each of the three intentions – specific, general, and attitudinal – you are moving from the fruits of presence to incarnating those graces in your actions and choices in your day. When the opportunities arise to perform them, you are moving not so much under your own "power," but under the grace of the Spirit. You are completing the task of God's interacting with and saving the world. No small task!

Evelyn Underhill, (1875–1941) an English Anglo-Catholic writer and pacifist known for her numerous works on religion and Christian mysticism, writes *"For [mystics,] contemplation and action are not opposites, but two interdependent forms of a life that is one – a life that rushes out to a passionate communion with the true and beautiful, only that it may draw from this direct experience of Reality a new intensity wherewith to handle the world of things; and remake it, or at least some little bit of it, 'nearer to the heart's desire.'"[77]

[77] Richard Rohr, "Mystics and Non-Dual Thinkers," *Richard Rohr's Daily Meditation*, August 9, 2015, http://myemail.constantcontact.com/Richard-Rohr-s-Meditation--Evelyn-Underhill.html?soid=1103098668616&aid=U4kuNaxATBY, (November 1, 2015).

WHAT GOES ON IN THE DARKNESS?

What takes place in the space between the individual in a state of awareness and the God who is awaiting him or her? Whatever it is, it is not conceptual, nor is it able to be put into words. We need to go to the affective level and express it in terms of feelings or images, poetry or metaphor. It has often been expressed in terms of the gaze an infant has of its mother's face when in her arms. Transfixed, the child's eyes are windows through which a presence is being conveyed, a presence deeper than words or thoughts, a presence that is tactile, affective, and unitive. It is the experience of the mystics who speak of spiritual betrothal and impassioned embrace. As we have said earlier, many have had spontaneous spiritual experiences in which they have seen or tasted the divine in their midst. So with the disposition of ourselves to gaze upon God's face and experience God's love for us, we are moved deeply by the abiding presence. The deepest longing of our heart is sated, if only for the briefest moment, but clearly the connection between longing and proper object of the longing meet and embrace. This is enough for us to know we have tasted that for which our heart longs.

A word needs to be said when this taste is not experienced, when all that is felt is absence, dryness, and waiting. Such moments can be useful, and the mystics speak often of such situations. At such times, it is helpful to simply surrender yourself to God. Another aid is spoken of by John of the Cross, who encourages us to remember that the one-inch of darkness just beneath the grass is a different quality of darkness than the darkness deep within the earth. The former is teaming with life and nutrients and ready to bring forth life, whereas the latter is deep, dark, and lifeless. Still, others are ready to say, *"Lord, I'm ready to be here with you; please calm my soul and quiet my spirit."*

Thomas Keating states that,

> It is important to realize that the place to which we are going
> is one in which the knower, the knowing, and that which is

71

known are all one. Awareness alone remains. This is what divine union is. There is no reflection of self. The experience is temporary, but it orients you toward the contemplative state. So long as you feel united with God, it cannot be full union. So long as there is a thought, it is not full union. The moment of full union has no thought. <u>You don't know about it until you emerge from it.</u> [emphasis added] In the beginning it is so tenuous that you may think you were asleep. It is not like the sense of felt union with the Lord that takes place on the level of self-reflection. Union on the spiritual level is the infusion of love and knowledge together, and while it is going on, it is non-reflective."[78]

Thinking, as we have mentioned before, can take many forms. Most of what is going on when we are thinking and trying to let go of it so we might rest with simple awareness is obvious as in, *"Oh, my mind is just wandering,"* or *"I am thinking about an emotion,"* or *"I have a breakthrough thought,"* or *"I am being reflective."* Thomas Keating lists a fifth kind of thinking that is not at first evident. He calls it "interior purification."[79] This sort of thought arises from the regular practice of Centering Prayer. It is able to purify the unconscious part of our deeper selves and to free us up for the fuller flow of grace. All the upsets relating to our family of origin could be contacted in this purification. Where sleep and resting does not have an impact on them, sitting in silence can, and it begins to lift the upsets, slowly at first, but at a greater rate, as commitment and time spent in contemplative silence increases. He suggests that simply accepting them without resistance is the best way to deal with them. As these once troublesome memories lift, we begin to see ourselves as less than stellar than we first thought in our kindness, generosity, or ability to listen. This inner awakening leads to transformation in how others, and

---

[78] Thomas Keating, *Open Mind, Open Heart*, op. cit. 69.
[79] Ibid., p.95.

we, see ourselves. This peace gives us greater courage to face the dark side of our personalities. So, emotionally-charged thoughts can have a transformative effect. Emotionally-charged thoughts are the chief way that the unconscious has of expelling chunks of emotional baggage. In this way, without our perceiving it, a great many emotional conflicts that are hidden in our unconscious and affecting our decisions more than we realize are being resolved. As a consequence, over a period of time, you will feel a greater sense of well-being and inner freedom. The very thoughts that you lament while in prayer are freeing the psyche from the damage that has accumulated in your nervous system over a lifetime. In this prayer both thoughts and silence have important roles to play.[80]

THE POWER OF PRESENCE

It has been said that the most popular religious depiction in Western Art is not of Jesus as the Good Shepherd, or of Jesus knocking at the door, or of Jesus in the Garden of Gethsemane, but of the Madonna and Child, the infant Jesus nestled in the arms of his mother, gazing upward into her eyes. If you place yourself into the work of art, you can begin to understand the power of the gaze. You begin to feel the presence of love and tenderness, of nurturance and support, of unconditional love, and how it is made manifest in the full and active engagement of all the senses, the scent of the mother, the support of her hands, the sweet taste of the milk of her breast, and perhaps deepest of all, the gaze fully fixed between them. They are both one in the presence of each other. It is no accident that those first few years of gazing and nurturing set the stage for a life of intimacy and unconditional love. Long before the infant possesses intellectual or cognitive intelligence, he or she is being grounded in emotional intelligence. Parenthetically, it is interesting to

---

[80] Thomas Keating, *Open Mind, Open Heart*, op.cit. 98-99.

note just how Da Vinci was able to have a more diminutive mother holding a larger-bodied son in her arms without the sculpture looking odd. It is also no small accident that the same depiction is portrayed in art at the end of Jesus' life, as he is taken down from the cross and laid in the arms of his mother, so beautifully depicted by Leonardo DaVinci in his Pietà.

Scientists used to hold that our brains use logical thought processes to interpret and predict other people's actions. However, views have changed, and many now believe that we understand others not by thinking, but by feeling. Mirror neurons formed by gazing let us simulate not only other peoples' actions, but the intentions and emotions behind those actions. Thus, when someone smiles, our mirror neurons for smiling are fired and are creating a sensation in our own mind of the feeling that comes with smiling. You don't have to think about what the other person intends by smiling. You experience the meaning immediately and effortlessly. So, the gaze of mother and child and child to mother becomes a pathway for the formation of such emotions as empathy, love, and joy. Mirror neurons allow us to receive and interpret facial expressions, such as a frown of disgust or a smile of love. The same regions of the brain of mother and child become activated.[81] When the gazings between mother and child have been plentiful, emotional intelligence is the result.

BECOMING WHOLE

Richard Rohr, being very Jungian, discusses three levels of consciousness to speak of how going deeper in consciousness can help you break through your ego, as that entity that keeps telling you who you are, to a deeper

---

[81] Society For Neuroscience. "Mirror, Mirror In The Brain: Mirror Neurons, Self-understanding And Autism Research," ScienceDaily, *http://www.sciencedaily.com/releases/2007/11/071106123725.htm* (accessed February 7, 2016).

personal unconsciousness that really is your shadow side.[82] See Figure #5: *"Individual, Personal, and Collective Unconscious."*

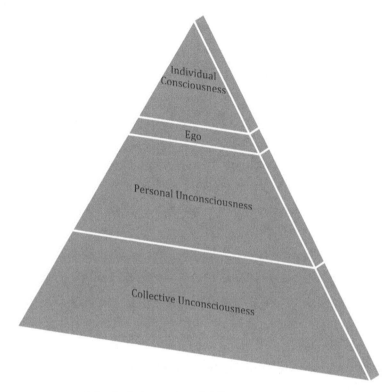

Individual, Personal, and Collective Unconscious

As you go deeper, you contact the very seat of your soul, the collective unconscious. The model helps us understand what goes on in contemplative prayer. As you let go of thinking and move to awareness, you shed the thinking self with all its judging, analyzing, noticing, and speculating. It is the ego that keeps us thinking. As you quiet your mind and enter the state of awareness, you are in touch with the shadow side of yourself, and here you realize that before God you are nothing and there is a sense that that is okay. You achieve a state of expressed wisdom

---

[82] Richard Rohr, *Things Hidden: Scripture as Spirituality,* (Cincinnati: St. Anthony Messenger Press, 2008), 75-76.

in such moments. There is little risk in being nothing, for you have come to see the ego for what it truly is, namely, highly protected, needing to be right and feeling important, and before God there is the added level of delight and abiding that is experienced. As you move through this state, you enter a collective unconscious where the experience is no longer *"I am nothing,"* but *"I am everything."* It is of its essence collective. This is a state of love and integration with the entire cosmos. Living out of this state, one does not respect the environment, eat nutritiously, care for others, or use resources responsibly because of any more urgings or moral codes, but simply because of the union one feels and experiences with all that is. It is here that you feel connected to everything and experience all of life as one. Rohr, along with Jung, would say this is what people would call the soul.

The bottom part of the triangle is the deep unconscious, or what Jung calls the collective unconscious. There you are connected to everything and experience things in their unity. The collective unconscious holds images that fascinate people in all cultures, across times and places. Jung calls these universal truths and symbols – that are just waiting to be revealed – archetypes or ruling images. Here Jung breaks significantly with Freud, who seems to think that sex or the pleasure principle underlies everything else. Jung, instead, believes that when you go deep enough, you will find the numinous, the God archetype, the place where you are complete and whole. This may be what most people think of as the soul.[83]

Contemplative Prayer Makes a Difference

When regular times devoted to contemplative prayer become habitual, and a regular time of day and format for spending twenty to thirty minutes in the presence is established, changes begin to take place in the

---

[83] Adapted from Richard Rohr, unpublished "Rhine" talks (2015).

life of the believer. At first, they are subtle and may go unnoticed by the one in prayer, but nevertheless slow incremental bearing of fruit from the presence begins to take place. At the purely human level, we may be gaining in patience at simply sitting still, appreciating the silence, learning to quiet the mind more easily, gaining a sense of balance, or becoming more grounded. At a deeper level, however, we are experiencing the fruits of gazing, of resting in God's arms, before God's face, and a flow back and forth is taking place. It is this flow that is the cause of a deeper life force of divine life that is of its very nature transformational. Over the years, I have experienced this flow and its resultant changes. At first, they were subtle, although friends and family members noticed a slowing of the speed of my speech. Then came an openness simply to listen to what another person was saying and not having to compete in telling my story or even worse, having to top theirs. As the longing for God's presence grew, so did the time spent in contemplative prayer. This time spent began to increase in duration and frequency. As it did, so did the fruits. One such fruit was a greater appreciation of the present moment, which went from the experience of it as a monotonous presence of waiting for something to happen to a desire to simply be or rest in the present moment. A second fruit was an openness to tasting and relishing whatever the moment was offering, whether it was an unexpected or undesired rain shower or an abrupt change in plans on the part of an individual of the group. There was growth in appreciating the very "is-ness" of what is because in the moment's experience, that is what was being offered. A third experience was an indifference as to what others might want to do or decide where to eat. It was not so much a disinterest, as it was a greater willingness to go along with the group. In the end, what did it matter beyond a fickle preference whether we went Italian, Chinese, or Mexican for dining? This was a noticeable change - both on my part, as it was in the perception of group members. Michael Brown, in his *The Presence Process*, has noted 44 fruits of being in the present moment, a state akin to contemplative presence. See Appendix D: *"Fruits of Awareness"* for a complete list of these.

His first ten include:

1. *We respond instead of reacting*
2. *We have more energy*
3. *We overcome procrastination*
4. *We complete tasks efficiently, effortlessly, and feel as though we have more time in which to accomplish them*
5. *We no longer hurry*
6. *Working conditions become more enjoyable*
7. *We are less resistant to the unpredictable currents of life*
8. *We experience spontaneous creativity*
9. *We feel more comfortable around our immediate family*
10. *Circumstances and people that once annoyed us no longer take up our attention*[84]

A New Learning Model

These changes and others like them had me beginning to wonder how might I get in front of the action and cooperate more actively and more consciously with God's grace and not simply wait for changes to occur and call them to mind after a year or two or have others notice them. What came to mind was the image of driving, and how we use the rear view mirror to see where we have been and the windshield to see where we are going is very appropriate. Using this analogy, I had come to realize the impact of contemplative prayer in my life by looking through the rear view mirror, as it were, to how I came to where I was. While I treasured the fruit of silence, I wanted to take more initiative in co-creating with God's grace. I wanted to drive by looking ahead through the windshield. It

---

[84] Michael Brown, *The Presence Process: A Healing Journey Into Present Moment Awareness,* (New York and Vancouver: Beaufort Books and Namaste Publishing, 2005), 244-249.

simply seemed more productive to drive looking through the windshield than sitting still and peering through the rear view mirror regarding how I had gotten to where I had landed. It was out of this perspective that the idea of experiential learning came to mind.

Many of us were raised on the pedagogy of the lecture method in school. The teacher stood before you and lectured for 45 minutes, a few questions were entertained and an assignment given, highlighting the material covered. You then gave her back the material she had given you, usually in a test or other evaluative setting. Experiential learning, on the other hand, had the individual listening to some instruction and immediately followed by an experiential application to one's life situation. Having had the experience, reflection on it followed with several specific questions and then a sharing - first in small groups of three or four, where it was easier to share personal information, and then in a larger group led by a teacher or facilitator. It was this model, applied to contemplative prayer, that set the course for getting in front of the action and having the action grow out of the experience of silent prayer with a level of intentionality, yet open completely to God's grace.

ANALOGY OF THE 2-SIDED COIN

Just as 2 tools, 2 obstacles, and 4 steps (2+2=4) was an easy way to remember the steps into contemplative prayer, an image was developed for a way of having that prayerful presence become contemplative *action*. The tool is the 2-sided coin. See Figure #6: *"The Analogy of the 2-Sided Coin."*

Every coin must have two sides and each of the two sides is complimentary and bears some relationship to the other. Thus, as a coin can be understood by looking at either side, with each side expressing a different aspect of the reality, so too can a contemplation "coin" be understood from either side of the "coin of contemplation." Thus far, we have considered the side called prayer. The obverse side let us call "action." Let us also say that both sides are individual expressions of the very same reality. They are simply different modes of being. Thus, the experience of the contemplative prayer alone must get expressed in some type of action. To have prayer isolated from action or its impact on my day could resort to a kind of navel gazing. On the other hand, to have faith-filled action without contemplation could degenerate into what can become meaningless activity. But together – the one in prayer disposing himself and God being fully present – each enhances the other, and God becomes visible in and through the one in prayer. It is these actions we will now consider. It will also allow us to get ahead of the action in order to play an important role in the area of intentionality and cooperating with grace to achieve God's will for me in my life.

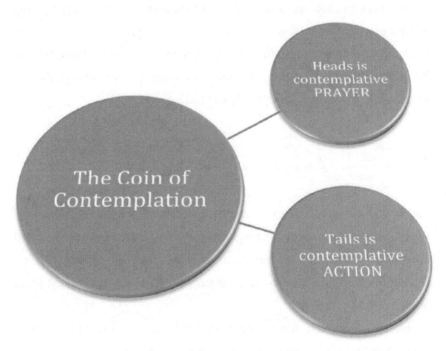

The Analogy of the 2-Sided Coin

THE POWER OF INTENTION

When you make an intention, you are using your will. Doing so is more than wishing or wanting or even praying for something. It is creating a sense of determination to make it happen. Your intention is a commitment to accomplishing an objective, to bring into being something that is not there to begin with, or to continue creating something that already is. The action that carries out the intention is not primary, but the unseen reason behind the action – the intention – is. True, you cannot see the intention, but the consequences and the experience are shaped by the intention, not by the action. As the source for action, the intention is the quality of consciousness that you bring to an action.[85]

An added benefit of an intention is, that once made, possibilities for fulfilling it begin to present themselves. It is as if the universe aligns itself to support your intention. When coming from contemplative prayer and moving to contemplative action – that is, action that is resourced or graced from the divine presence – how I shape my intention is very important. I would want to shape it with respect to the experience of God's presence that I had in the silence. Reflecting on the experience before the face of God, that experience will be without ego, without past trauma or future fears. It will be one of fullness and joy in the presence. We must remember that during the silence, thinking was eschewed and awareness espoused so God could be as God is in God's manifestation to us. In short, then, the quality of the intention I make will flow from the quality of my awareness of God.

A second important point needs to be made regarding intentions and actions. We know from brain science that if you were to ask me to wiggle the index finger of my right hand, that in order to do so the prefrontal lobe of my brain would be activated. If that part of my brain had been damaged in some way and you would ask me to wiggle my index finger,

---

[85] Gary Zukav and Linda Francis, *The Mind of the Soul*, (New York: Free Press, 2003).

I would be able to consider your request but would be unable to carry it out. The interesting thing is that if I make only an intention to do it, while I am not yet carrying it out into action, even then the same lobe of my prefrontal cortex would be activated, although not to the same degree. What this implies is the important role that intention plays, not only to create the action, but to serve as a bit of a dress rehearsal to it - getting me primed to do it and thus making it easier to do when the action is willed.[86] Thus, if I am committed to jogging every morning as my daily exercise routine and committed to my health - making the intention before going to bed and putting out my running shoes and gear next to my bed - I am creating an intention that will have an important effect when I arise and perhaps not feel like running. I have created optimal conditions for doing so no matter how drowsy or tired I may feel at that moment. Yes, acting through an intention, the universe does seem to align itself with you, and a task becomes easier. Try laying out a large task, or writing out or thinking through something you need to do tomorrow that you do not relish or enjoy doing. Walk through a task that seems overwhelming at the moment, e.g., tax preparation, a lecture you are to give, moving, planning a holiday dinner, preparing for Christmas, etc., to experience the power of intention.

DESCRIBING THE EXPERIENCE

For one person, the 20 or 30 minutes will be experienced as passing very slowly, while for another it will have flown by. Both spent the same time being still, so what then accounts for the two different experiences? In English, we have only one word for "time," and that is "time." However, the more words a language has for something, the more nuanced the words can be, thus the Swedes are said to have 25 words for snow, each

---

[86] Andrew Newberg, M.D. and Mark Robert Waldman, *How God Changes Your Brain*, (New York: Ballantine Books, 2009).

word nuancing a different aspect of the reality. Thus, there is a Swedish word for wet-slushy snow, snow in snowdrifts, compacted hard snow, artificial snow, snow at Christmas, frozen carbon dioxide, snow mixed with rain, etc. Unlike us, but not as nuanced as the Swedes, the Greeks, we saw above, actually had two words for time. One was *"chronos,"* which meant moment-by-moment time. It's experienced as clock-watching slow time, as a student in an uninteresting class or lecture or proverbially, *"watching the pot boil."* The other word the Greeks had for time was *"kairos,"* which signified a time lapse, a moment in which everything seemed to happen. What is happening when speaking of *kairos* depends on the individual who is using it. *Chronos* is more quantitative, while *kairos* is qualitative and permanent. Applied to how the time in prayer was experienced, we could say that if it was *chronos* for us, we were probably thinking or were distracted. If it was *kairos,* we were in awareness where there was no time, only presence and connectedness to the other. It was engagement as something one does, but passive resting in, savoring, soaring, floating, and being in God. With practice at disposing yourself to God's presence and becoming better at quieting the mind, awareness will increase, and the feeling that time has flown by will increasingly become your experience.

As a way of considering contemplative prayer in relationship to contemplative action, think once again of the hand modeling we have done before with the opened palm of the right hand moving toward the opened palm of the left hand and meeting it in chapter 2. Figure #7: *"Model of Contemplative Prayer and Contemplative Action"* illustrates both the movement into prayer and the movement out to action.

This is analogous to the state of awareness and the experience of union that comes with it. For the contemplation to action analogy, turn the right hand outward and move it away from the left. As it goes, it takes with it the experience of the "dusting" of the presence. So, the first thing to do after sitting in silence for 20 or 30 minutes is to ask, *"What was the experience like?"* or, better still, *"What did the experience feel like?"* It is important to remember that we are not looking for conceptual explanations here. It will be more of an affective description of the experience, such as deep satisfaction, or a sense of being held or treasured, or it might have been a sense of tranquility or peace I have never felt before. It is understandable that the time spent may on occasion be painfully distracting or filled with compulsive thinking or dark thoughts. At such times, it is better to begin with meditating on a scene from the Gospel or a Psalm passage that is more uplifting and taking a sacred word or mantra from it to dispose yourself to the presence.

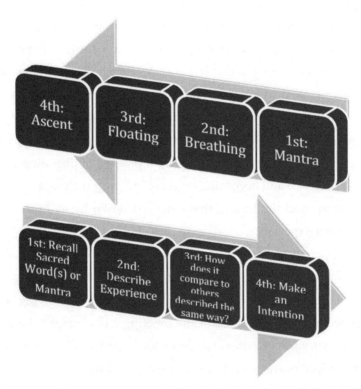

Model of Contemplative Prayer and Contemplative Action

When describing your experience of the silence, a specific follow-up question will always be helpful. Allow me to explain. Let us say that you would describe the experience as comforting and warm. The follow-up question would be, "How does this experience of "comforting and warm" compare with other similar experiences where you have felt the same way?" That other experience may have been a snowy night at a ski lodge last winter or sitting in front of a fire in the fireplace at home with the family. The reason for the follow-up question is to compare how the two different experiences described by the same word or words satisfied. It is most probable that the contemplative one will have been deeper, fuller, more satisfying. If this be so, then there would be more of a tendency to return to contemplative presence the next time. What is really at work here, of course, is that the deepest longing of our hearts is being met in the divine presence and that all other similar experiences will pale by comparison. A little exercise to further study these kinds of comparisons would be to create a 5x7 table. In the first column, list the mantra used for prayer, and in the second column, list the adjectives that described your experience of contemplative presence each day. In the third column, list prior experiences that could be described with similar feelings and emotions. And finally, reflect on the preference and why. See Appendix E: "Comparing Similar Experiences of Satisfaction" for a template of the chart.

Types of Intentions

To build on the 2-sided coin analogy, the description of the experience becomes the topside of the coin. The bottom side of the coin becomes an intention I make of how to cooperate with the grace of God's presence that I have received. It should be kept in mind that in reality it is all God's grace – experiencing his presence and being able to act out of God's presence. We cooperate with it, and this cooperation is a source of our dignity and honor. So how might this cooperation be realized by the one praying? We do it the way we perform other such tasks, namely by stating an intention and then targeting a way of realizing that intention. Actions that are realized as part of a larger goal or effort need both an intention and a way of realizing that intention. In this way, the larger goal or purpose is achieved. It is no less so regarding God's plan for us through our participation in God's presence and then our cooperation with God's plan.

An intention is a state of mind that expresses a commitment to carrying out an action in the future. When an intention flows from the grace of God's presence, it becomes part of a larger drama that includes God, others, and us. So, intention both ties us into a larger plan or goal, and it is the precursor for effective action. In addition, if I make an intention to do something, my brain is scanning at different levels of consciousness and is on the lookout for the intention to be realized. So, I may be under the influence of grace without even knowing it. We will see in chapter 4 what the significance in the action that is finally realized may be. It may not be what we intended. How to know whether it was God's will or not will also be discussed. For now, it is enough to know the power of intention for accomplishing an act.

When I reflect on God's presence in prayer and come out of that time spent in silence, my experience is usually one of great satisfaction, feeling loved, luminescent with a glow from within, calm or grounded. These are just a few effects that come to mind; there are others. If any one of these is the topside of my coin, I could have a multitude of intentions regarding any one of them. The intentions can be one of three types: attitudinal, general, or specific. What might be some intentions that I could make from any of them? For example, if it is great satisfaction, the intention might be to eat my three meals today more slowly and continue to enjoy the satisfaction I received from God's presence. This would be a specific intention. If it is feeling loved, I might make an intention to call someone I have not been solicitous of in recent times. This is a general intention. If it is feeling luminescent, perhaps I could make an intention to take time to better understand something that has caught my attention and Google it later. Another specific intention. And if it is calm or tranquility that describes my presence, then it may be wearing a face of calmness throughout the day and leave it to God to place others in my path to experience. This would be an example of an attitudinal intention.

In all cases, we can see how the divine presence can make a difference in me, and from within me, to others. Here we have an effective connection between the divine and the human through my own mediation. It is the best of bringing the grace of God to others. One thing should be clearly understood: that in the moment, when I am carrying out my intention, it would serve me well, by affirming the grace of God within me, that it is not I who is actually performing the action, but God's grace through me. As stated in Ephesians, *"I became a servant of this gospel by the gift of God's grace given me through the working of his power."*[87] Another is that whatever the intention – attitudinal, general, or specific – grace can be operating consciously or unconsciously. The fruits – either good or bad – will determine whether it was God's grace or ego during the action.

One might ask, why make the distinction at all? We will see later that it could be helpful to note over many days of such intentions what types of intentions we lean toward and how we might make efforts to diversify to experience the benefits of the variety. It may also be a gentle nudge from God to seek new avenues through which to actualize God's grace. Each of the types of intentions is grace operative, each having a different impact on ourselves or others, where attitudinal primarily affects us: specific, a single person and general, a small or large group. In these ways, the analogy of the coin helps us go from individual presence to a world beyond, acting out of God's grace through our own cooperation.

CONTEMPLATIVE ACTION AS THE FRUIT OF CONTEMPLATIVE PRAYER

We have seen how we might cooperate with grace after having spent some time in contemplative prayer. Think of it as the mystery of moving from the sea of silence to the arena of action. Very instructive in this regard is

---

[87] Eph. 3:7.

Evelyn Underhill cited above.[88] In her later writing, Underhill focused on uniting contemplation and action, drawing on the grace of God's presence to make it operative through her own choices. She writes, *"Try to arrange things so that you can have a reasonable bit of quiet every day and do not . . . think it selfish . . . You are obeying God's call and giving Him [sic] the opportunity to teach you what He wants you to know, and so make you more useful to Him and to other souls."*[89] And she adds, in line with Keating's understanding of how God works through five kinds of thinking, *"Remember God is acting on your soul all the time, whether you have spiritual sensations or not."*[90] When it comes to making concrete intentions regarding our daily lives, she counsels, *"Take the present situation as it is and try to deal with what it brings you, in a spirit of generosity and love. God is as much in the difficult home problems as in the times of quiet and prayer.... Try especially to do His will there, deliberately seek opportunities for kindness, sympathy, and patience."*[91]

When we abide in silence, when we rest silently in God, we are able to experience several fruits of the Holy Spirit, which can be listed as the 3G's:

➢ *Gratitude* for the present moment: that is, an awareness of the presence within the moment

➢ *Generosity* of spirit toward others: less judging and labeling of others, less reactivity, and more compassion

➢ *Guidance* as intuitively knowing: what to do and not to do, what to say and not to say, what to incorporate and what to let go.

We bridge the gap from contemplative prayer to contemplative action through the use of the coin where God's grace experienced is then re-created through my intention, which serves as a prelude to action.

[88] Evelyn Underhill, *The Letters of Evelyn Underhill* edited by Charles Williams, (Harlow: Longmans, Green and Co.: 1944).

[89] Evelyn Underhill, *The Letters of Evelyn Underhill*, op. cit., 141.

[90] Evelyn Underhill, *The Mount of Purification* (Harlow: Longmans, Green and Co., 1949), 184.

[91] Evelyn Underhill, *The Letters of Evelyn Underhill*, op. cit. 137.

A Simple Journaling

Journaling seems to be something you either love or hate. In retreat ministry, I have found women tend to favor journaling more than men. There seems to be an aversion men have to writing down their thoughts or experiences. Those who are inclined to write down their thoughts and feelings say it helps them clarify what is going on in their minds. The writing gives them substance, and they see them as words and phrases they have created. Others, as noted, find the activity burdensome. Hope is at hand. Long paragraphs of internal dialogue, lengthy descriptions of the setting, or endless descriptions of how you see things are not primary in recording contemplative prayer and contemplative actions. I will not be suggesting that anyone write paragraphs of reflection on their prayer experiences. I will, however, suggest a cryptic noting down of three items after each daily session of contemplative prayer.

First, the one or two words that served as the sacred word(s) for that day. Second, a single short phrase that describes the experience. Keep in mind that it will be the description of an experience so the words will be of the affective domain, as in, *"It felt like standing under a refreshing waterfall,"* or *"I felt as if I were taken up in God's arms and was very safe,"* etc. Third, state an intention – either attitudinal, general, or specific – of how the experience may have an impact today in your life, given where you will be going, what you will be doing, and with whom. That is it – three short cryptic elements of your 20 or 30 minutes of silence. If you find a longer, more complete list of questions helpful, the following is offered:

> ➢ What did I choose as shimmering phrase or sacred word?
> ➢ Did the session of silence go fast or slow?
> ➢ How would I describe those 20 minutes?
> ➢ How was this experience different from other experiences described with the same word or words?

➢ How did I deal with thinking that came up or distractions that would not go away?

➢ How might this experience be lived out in my choices today?

Whether you use the three simple questions or the preceding longer list of six, to help you do this in a more organized fashion, Appendix F: *"Weekly Contemplation Log"* is a weekly chart for the recording of the three elements for each of the seven days. This weekly sheet will be very important in chapter 4 where you begin to look at your prayer over the course of a week, or month, or several months and see how God is drawing you forward into transformation. To see how contemplative presence can be translated into effective action that makes a difference is not so much using your willpower as a "muscle," but rather acting in and through the grace of presence.

The New You

In addition to many of the fruits of being in the present moment and aware of God's presence to me, friends and family have noted other subtle changes. Among them, they tell me I appear quieter, more settled and grounded; talk more slowly; listen better; am more attentive to what's going on around me; seem to depend on intuition or "a feel" for things; no longer imbibe spirits or collect coupons, have lower blood pressure, am maintaining a good weight for my height and body build; and am more faithful to daily exercise and contemplative prayer. A most noteworthy thing is that I no longer seem to have a preference for where we vacation, the cuisine of the restaurant where we eat, or what time we leave for an event. It is often surprising to see the number of books, clothes, and savings I find myself giving to those in need. Coming from a richer center has impacted my life in so many ways. I am reminded of Thomas Keating's statement regarding what takes place in the presence, beneath the conscious or cognitive level. God's grace is active and alive, touching our very souls in ways we have not yet imagined. This chapter has attempted to augment that silent presence of God's working within me, beneath the level of my own consciousness with intentionality and a sense of purpose.

Jesus admonishes us to abide in his love.[92] It is for Christians, the great commandment. It is in contemplative prayer that awareness becomes the occasion for God's self-manifestation to us as mystical love. As our longing for God is fulfilled in such presence, we become the very love we experience. This empowers us not only to be instruments of love to others and to see love and goodness where we had not seen it before, but abiding in peace within, we will begin to see peace outside ourselves as well. Abide in beauty within, and we will see beauty outside ourselves. The experience of remaining or abiding moves religion from the esoteric realms of the doctrinal stratosphere - where it has been for many. Living out of the presence requires no moral codes beyond being a loving person in mind and heart.

---

[92] John 15:4-5.

CHAPTER

4

TRACKING AND DISCERNMENT

WHAT IS THE CONTEMPLATION LOG?

The question arises as to what sort of impact might the effect of repeatedly spending time in contemplative presence have on the one who prays. That is, as God is encountered, with nothing added on the part of the one who prays, and as intentions to do good out of that experience of grace are made, what changes in behavior, attitude, or relationships might accrue? To begin to pay attention to these changes, we need to consider the idea of tracking.

Tracking has four important aspects, of which we have already considered the first three in chapter 3. The first is writing down the short mantra that was used, and the second is recording a short description of your experience in prayer. The third is the intention you are making for the day that will flow from your experience. When we described this earlier, we used the image of a 2-sided coin as an easy way to remember it. Fourth, a new concept, which I will introduce now, is seeing how the intention was realized in actuality, that is, in the course of the day.

For example, I may have described my prayer experience as a *"loving embrace"* and made an intention to *"call a member of my family with whom I've had a misunderstanding."* However, in the course of the day, many unforeseen events thwarted the realization of my intention, but I was able to spend some time with a co-worker in the lunchroom with whom some distance in the relationship had developed recently. Whether I called the family member or chatted with the co-worker is not as important as the fact that I was acting under the experience of grace received in my Morning Prayer. I am always open to leave it to God's will that a different situation presents itself. It is important for tracking purposes to record *both* the intended thing and the actual thing that was done. This recording of the actual thing done is written onto the table the next morning and before you begin your prayer session for that day. See Appendix F: *"Weekly Tracking Chart"* for an illustration of a series of Sacred Words, Descriptions of Presence, Intentions, and Actions over several days. A blank sheet with seven rows for the days of the week follows for copying. Notice that the blank sheet lists the date of the week and the page number so the sheets can be hole-punched and placed in a binder. Next, we will offer some thoughts on how to analyze the sheets and determine how God and God's grace may be changing you.

We may remember from elementary school that it takes three points to demonstrate a pattern., e.g., the even numbers of 2,4,6. Just two numbers will not give you much. It should be remembered, however, that some patterns or trends cannot be demonstrated even with three points and that the more points, the greater the accuracy of the pattern being correct. Two points might signal a trend upwards, but how could you be sure that it is linear or exponential? And while a third point could give additional information, a fourth or a fifth one would be most helpful to draw any real conclusions. I would like to apply the same analytical measuring rod to the daily impact our contemplative prayer may be having on our personal transformation. Such a practice has been revelatory for my own sessions of prayer. The "revelations" came after tracking or keeping track of daily statements of intention and how those intentions were actualized over the course of a month.

ANALYZING A MONTH'S PRAYER, INTENTIONS, AND ACTIONS

Having accumulated a month's worth of sacred words, descriptions, intentions, and actions, you can then begin analyzing each of the columns presented in Figure #8: Tracking Contemplative Actions.

			S I S			Action (Recorded the next morning when preparing that day's "Phrase that shimmers")
	My Contemplative Living (Contemplation → Action) For the Week of _____, Page ____					
Date	Phrase That Shimmers	Sacred Word(s)	S I S	Description of the Experience	Intention (Attitudinal, General, Specific)	
	"Surrender to God and he will give you all you need"	Surrender / receive		Trust	Remain open to whatever the Lord presents to me today (Attitudinal)	Picked up trash along the jogging route
	"Deny yourself, pick up your cross and follow me"	Deny / follow		Freedom	Prayerfully listening at our committee meeting today (General)	Was able to build on the parts of a proposal I agreed with
	"Abide in me and I in you"	Bonded		Oneness	Conversation with a friend during our drive to a meeting (Specific)	Openness to a drawn out conversation in car and over dinner

Tracking Contemplative Actions

Let us begin by noting the sacred word(s) column for patterns or exceptions. For example, do you tend to favor the use of words that shimmer, images, movements, or gestures as a way of disposing you for contemplative presence? If words are used most often, are they usually taken from Psalms, Gospels, or Epistles? As a suggestion, you might try using your less-favored practices to see if new ways to enter the presence are beckoning you.

In looking analytically at your month's intentions, are they more attitudinal, generic, or specific? Attitudinal intentions tend to open you up more to God presenting how they will be realized. That does not mean that generic or individual ones are less important. After all, a specific intention could well heal a relationship or offer someone mercy or forgiveness, or help a particular person in your life. From this vantage point, the generic intention would perhaps offer the benefits of both being open to whatever the Lord sends you, yet shaping that future just a bit by focusing on the grace received in prayer. The fruits of such analysis and noticing are excellent items to share with your spiritual director or spiritual guide. Perhaps the most significant observation, however, will come from looking down the last column of "actualizations." It could be enlightening to ask the question, *"How is the grace of contemplative presence affecting God's will in my life over the past month?"* Our intentions and how they compare to the actualizations can become the foundation for meaningful discernment.

Another fruitful way to approach tracking would be to consider Michael Brown's 44 Fruits that come from being present to the moment. These are listed in Appendix H: *"44 Fruits and Flowers of Present Moment Awareness."* In reviewing them, you would ask which one or two fruits would be desirable to experience in your own life and then choose scripture passages, poems, or songs that relate to that fruit. Create mantras from those and take them to deep breathing and the act of sitting in silence. Reflection on the quiet time will be the result of your brush with divine presence and can then be shaped into an intention that is more in line with what you would like to achieve. I find it helpful after my Morning Prayer time to jot my intention on a post-it and mount it on my laptop so I have a ready reminder of how I'm intending to live out my contemplative presence.

Once we have a sense of how our prayer, intentions, and actions are tracking, it is important to know something about discernment, that is, proven ways of reading and understanding how God interacts with us so our understanding may be clearer and possible outcomes more effective. We will now turn to two authors, one contemporary, Rose Mary Dougherty, and one more classical, St. Ignatius of Loyola, for their thoughts on discerning God's will.

DISCERNMENT ACCORDING TO ROSE MARY DOUGHERTY

There is a distinction between an act of discernment and the habit of discernment. We want to open discernment-as-a-habit up as a way of life, a flow of life. Rosemary Dougherty makes the distinction between discerning with regard to a specific choice (act) and being open to and responding to the myriad ways God leads us (habit.)[93] "Decisional Discernment," or discernment done to reach a decision, is the practice of viewing all of one's life through the eyes of faith and in that faith-stance noticing the movements of the heart to determine which of these movements is leading to greater love and authenticity. Questions for noticing this are: *"Where is my heart?"* and *"How does this fit with my heart's desire?"* It requires deliberation, e.g., Switch parishes? Retire now or later? What ministry should I pursue in retirement? In such cases, you need time to think about what God wants you to do. It is a process of considering both options and seeing what is going on inside you in terms of feelings and resistances regarding each. This type of discernment is for people trying to learn God's hopes and dreams for their lives.

Discernment as a habit, or as Dougherty calls it, *"Habitual Discernment"* is the attitude of listening to God in all of life, *"listening with the ear of the heart,"* as St. Benedict says. God is actively and caringly involved with us in every moment of our lives, even the most mundane of moments. God is not only present, but guides us to authentic expression of God's

---

[93] Rose Mary Dougherty, *Discernment: a path to spiritual awakening,"* (Mahwah: Paulist Press, 2009), 5-9.

presence with us in each moment. The habit of discernment finely tunes the ear of the heart so that we hear more clearly the invitation to love, and our choices are refined by this invitation to love. The important thing is not really the decision, but the process of opening to God through the decision and the learning that takes place in the process.

Nurturing discernment as a habit comes about through contemplative prayer, which nourishes our attentiveness by the time that we set aside on a regular basis simply to be with God. Such contemplative practices bring us to our center, where we live more fully in the present moment and are better able to hear our personal truth and authenticity. Prayerful reflection at the end of our day is fostered so we can be aware of the ways God has been present for us. One can experience a greater freedom for love and for inner freedom. As we grow in God's grace, our longing for God becomes greater than our longing for anything else.

Mystics speak of two effects of such presence: first that one comes to know that he or she is nothing before God, and that is called wisdom. Yes, we have been opened by awareness in God's presence to see ourselves just as we are and before God that is nothing. Yet, we do not despair because the very presence of God, as God is, not as we had imagined him in the past, becomes a consoling and merciful presence. Second, as we gaze at God, abide in God, we can look at others and still keep looking at God. We detach from our former ways of seeing our friends and what we want for them. It is resting in the divine presence that the individual comes to know that he or she is everything and that is love. Moving and living out of that presence creates the miracles of transformation in the one who prays. Love is no longer a "muscle" to be exercised and flexed, but a disposition, a point of view, a way of seeing the world. And it is by God's grace of that presence that we are able to do what we do.

In habitual discernment, our intention is either implicit or explicit to be free for God, free for love. To be free for love is to possess that inner freedom where the longing we speak of is greater than that for anything else. It is a freedom where we let go of our need to control things and to fall into the total freedom of loving and trusting God with all aspects of our life. Contemplative prayer has helped us take time to notice what gets in the way of being free, what hooks us, what takes us off track.

By the interplay of prayer and action and consciously choosing what gives us lasting satisfaction, as well as noting what gets in the way, we begin to appreciate Dougherty's comment in her work *"Discernment,"* where she says, *"This discernment that I speak of is a gift that has been given all of us. We don't create it; we don't receive it from someone. Perhaps we might say that we uncover it and nourish it. We uncover the gift and then we nourish it through the skillful means of noticing, through our prayer and through our growing openness to God in all of life."*[94] The "noticing" is critical. Reflection on what you are noticing is also important. Thus, it is possible on your tracking sheet either to ask yourself, *"What is God's plan for me regarding my primary relationships?"* or to ask, *"Where does my prayer seem to be leading me in general?"* Such questions serve well in selecting Psalms or scripture passages from which come phrases that shimmer and mantras.

Discernment According to Ignatius of Loyola

Ignatius of Loyola, the founder of the Jesuits, is perhaps the central figure when it comes to a method for discerning God's will. His "method" was developed out of his own experience of conversion and how God was leading him. The entire process from courtier and soldier to saint was written down and has come to us in his autobiography. After being wounded by a French cannonball at the Battle of Pamplona on May 20, 1521, one of Ignatius' legs was broken and the other seriously injured. He returned to the castle and had surgery performed on him without the benefit of anesthesia. During his nine-month recuperation period, he was reading *On the Life of Christ* and was moved by the lives of many saints

---

[94] Rose Mary Dougherty, *Discernment,* op. cit., 6.

and Fathers of the Church portrayed in that work. He slowly began to realize that the joy he received from imagining himself as a St. Francis or a St. Dominic was much more fulfilling and lasting than the joys of nightlife and courtship enjoyed previously, and so, he moved closer and closer toward imitating lives of sanctity. This moving closer to imitating those lives came to be known as the discernment of spirits or the path of consolations. As such, discernment in this case is the regular looking at those experiences that give you lasting and satisfying consolation and contrasting them with those that do not quite make the mark. As you keep moving forward by making choices in favor of the consolation, the path taken strengthens and is experienced as more life-giving.

In this very movement, Ignatius does state that there will also be desolations or letdowns. It is precisely in the discerning of good or evil spirits in either that one gains some surety in following the path that is God's will for you. Because we are given a very special longing for God as we come forth from the birth canal, and because nothing will satisfy this longing quite like its proper object for which it was created – namely God – lesser objects like possessions, money, titles, power, or success will pale before the acquiring of God himself.

Ignatius addresses three methods of discernment, but before considering each in some detail, it is important to review seven tenets that he offers the seeker before venturing into a specific method to determine whether something is of God or not. His seven tenets before discerning God's will are:

1. *Do not consider something manifestly evil*
2. *If you have already made an "unchangeable" decision, you should stick with it. And if you have made a "changeable" decision for good reasons and you are comfortable with it and there's no reason to change things, do not bother making a new decision*
3. *If it is not something that requires a decision, do not waste your time. You have already made a commitment*

4. *If you have made a good decision and suddenly feel downcast, it is not a sign to reconsider*

5. *When you have made a good decision to serve God better and after a while go into desolation, you should not change the decision; it is hardly a good spirit moving you*

6. *When you are feeling down, you would do well to pray a little more and increase the help you give to others*

7. *If you have made a changeable decision in a bad way, you can revisit it. You might want to make it anew in a properly ordered way. Why not take a fresh look at things?*[95]

To the discernment of spirits, which Ignatius experienced during his recuperation, he eventually added two other types of coming to know God's will. The first I call *"The Aha! Experience."* It is where the question and the answer come to the believer at once. There is no question about what to do. The decision comes without doubting or being able to doubt. For example, when you see someone in distress, you move immediately to action to save, protect, or care for the individual. There is no deliberation, *"Should I help the elderly woman who fell?"* or *"Should I run after that child that has wandered into the street alone?"*

The second type, we just spoke of, discernment of spirits, I would call moving from consolation to consolation. It is less clear than the first and would require some deliberation. It is a thoughtful consideration of which option before you offers you the greater consolation. One looks at the feelings and motions within as a sign that God is helping you with your choice. Here in a moment of decision, consolation is a sense of peace and of rightness regarding the choice, for God works through our deepest longings. When we are following that path to God, things intuitively just seem right. Things feel in synch because they are in synch! Just as St. Ignatius moved to greater acts of love and service and away from

---

[95] James Martin, SJ, *The Jesuit Guide to (Almost) Everything,"* (San Francisco: HarperOne, 2012), 311-312.

nightlife, a military career, and service in the Spanish court, so too can we move from a former style of life regarding possessions, power, and entitlement to simplicity, humility, and deference. As one moves along the path of consolations, that is, experiencing those small actions that satisfy the deeper longing for God, the individual is sure to encounter desolations. As we have seen above, desolation is anything that moves you toward hopelessness. So for Ignatius, while recovering after the Battle of Pamplona and reading the lives of the saints, he felt consolation, but desiring to impress the ladies now brought him desolation.

For the third type of discernment, or as Ignatius called them *"3 situations,"* I would use a phrase that is more contemporary, namely *"Force Field Analysis."* Here you find yourself with two or more good alternatives, but neither one is the obvious choice. There is no "Aha!" Moment, nor is there any clarity from prayer. In this third type of discernment, Ignatius provides two methods. The First Method is for those who like moving with their logical left-brain, as it is based on reason. Here he suggests that the individual begin with indifference, that is, to be open to either alternative or at least desire to be so. Second, as a seeker you put yourself in prayer regarding the choice, e.g., to buy or not to buy the house – and identify your ultimate objective. For Ignatius, that objective had become to please God. Third, you ask God to help move your heart toward the better decision. Fourth, make a list of positive and negative outcomes of the first option. Then make one for the second option. Each option will, of course, be a mixed bag. Fifth, Ignatius advises the individual to pray about them and see toward which alternative your reason is inclined to move. You will come to a choice eventually that will bring peace. Sixth, you finally ask God for some sort of confirmation outside yourself.

The Second Method under this third type of discernment relies more on imagination and right-brain use than on reason. Here you first imagine a person whom you have never met, and you create a narrative around the advice you would give this person. You then fast-forward to five years in the future and imagine how you might feel now after five years have elapsed regarding the decision you made. Continuing the fast-forward, you now imagine yourself at the point of death – morbid, yes, but clarifying nonetheless – and ask yourself, *"What should I have done?"* From the deathbed, Ignatius would have you move to imagine yourself at the Last Judgment and asking which choice would you want to offer God. Father Jim Martin in *The Jesuit Guide to (Almost) Everything"*[96] adds a fourth question for self-examination: *"Imagine what your best self would do."*[97] On occasion, I have employed both the second and third types of discernment and spent some time imagining living with each choice for a set period of time and seeing which choice gives me a greater sense of peace. In comparing the two situations, advantages and disadvantages have become clearer. It was while making a 30-day Ignatian Retreat many years ago at the Jesuit Retreat Center of Los Altos in Los Altos, California that I was introduced to Ignatius' means of discernment that I came to understand how powerful these methods were for coming to know God's will for me.

CONTEMPLATIVE ACTION AND DISCERNMENT

PERSONAL REFLECTION ON A MONTH'S TRACKING

Several things could be observed as the days passed into weeks and the weeks into a month. I became more comfortable with the sitting and with the silence. The longing for that quiet time each day began to grow. If an occasion arose where I was not able to take or make the time, I felt diminished, less grounded than I did when the time was made for prayer. Second, my intentions were not always realized as they had originally been stated. There were surprises in how some specific intentions were not realized and instead were fulfilled.

---

[96] Ibid., 325.
[97] Ibid.

For example, on one occasion with the sacred words *"surrender, receive,"* the experience of prayer was described at *"trustful and safe,"* and the intention was *"to remain open to whatever the Lord presents to me today."* The action that was recorded the next morning when preparing that day's phrase that shimmers was that I felt moved to pick up trash along the highway where I was doing my daily run that morning. This was something I would normally not have done, being taught as a child that it was not safe to pick up possible germ-infested trash. So, what began as an attitudinal intention was completed as a specific action.

Another example was the use of a general intention. The sacred word was *"Deny...surrender,"* and the intention made was to listen prayerfully to whatever was being said at a meeting I was to attend later in the day. The intention kept me open and noticing what each speaker was saying, and I was able to build on the parts of a proposal that I agreed with and, thus, move things forward, rather than simply speaking against the idea presented.

A final example of what would be called a specific intention was a result of the words for prayer of *"You and me."* The experience was a sense of oneness, closeness, and intimacy. My specific intention was to be attentive to expressing myself deeply and intimately in the conversation I was to have with a friend during our drive to a meeting that we were attending. The openness deepened our conversation in the car and continued it even through our dinner together.

It is important to note that whether or not the intention remained the same is not of great importance. What is important is how the *action* may have changed. If it changes regularly, then the change should be noted, and we should shift the type of intention we have been making (attitudinal, general, or specific) to the kind of action that keeps getting expressed. So, if you tend to make attitudinal intentions that get expressed specifically, then begin making more specific intentions. On the other hand, if specific intentions continually get expressed as a general attitude, then move to making your intentions increasingly attitudinal. This seems to be an effective way of getting your choices in line with where the Spirit is calling you. A second item of importance is the effect you are having on relationships with others, that is, what the impact of your prayer and actions coming from that prayer are having not only on yourself, but on how others perceive you. These changes, though small or unnoticed at first, will begin to have an impact on you and your family, on your friends, and associates at work.

Finally, the important thing to recognize is that the actions that flow from your intentions are movements of the Spirit within you, so the actual doing of them is as much God's Spirit as it is you, the doer. You are becoming more the instrument in God's hands, accomplishing good in the world. For this reason, some of the surprises in the contrast between your intention and the actual action may be things you might never have been able to accomplish on your own without the prayer and grace of presence, things like forgiving a horrific deed done to you, speaking to someone you have not said a word to in years, or coming to peace with someone who has died. In experiencing empowerment regarding such hurdles, I am reminded of the antiphon: *"Their own strength could not save them; it was your strength and the light of your face."*[98]

In Colossians we read, *"Since, then, you have been raised with Christ, set your hearts on things above, where Christ is, seated at the right hand of God. Set your minds on things above, not on earthly things. For you died, and your life is now hidden with Christ in God. When Christ, who is your life, appears, then you also will appear with him in glory.*[99] Contemplative prayer not only sets our hearts on "things above," and its repetition helps us die to things that attract but do not satisfy, it also gives us a taste of the glory to come and serves as a kind of power drink of grace to move us to act. Watching and noticing those actions helps put us in touch with God's will for us. For Dame Gascoigne, the grace of presence is already there. It simply needs to be realized and brought into action.

---

[98] The Divine Office, Antiphon of Matins, December 24, 2015.

[99] Col. 3:1-4.

One thing alone I crave (excerpt)

One thing alone I crave
namely
All is everything

This One
I seek
the only One
do I desire
....
What or Who this One is
I may not say
can never feel
Nothing
more or less
is there to say

For the One is not simply in all
the One Being is over all

YOU are my GOD
holding me
within my very SELF[100]

BEGINNING WITH THE END IN MIND

There is another way to allow God's grace to move us in new directions
of transformation other than the one we have been considering, which

---

[100] Dame Catherine Gascoigne, "One Thing Alone I Crave" in Housden, Roger, *For
Lovers of God Everywhere*, (Carlsbad: Hay House, 2009), 48.

has been mantra → experience → intention → action. This additional way is to look at how others have been transformed by presence and see which of those might be something called for in your own life as a seeker or disciple. As a starting point, Michael Brown's effects of practicing the presence could serve as an appropriate wish list.[101] For the sake of example, let us look at his first three suggestions:

1. We respond instead of react
2. We have more energy
3. We overcome procrastination

If it is responding rather than reacting, what might be the virtue or characteristic of the disciple that would help us do that? Might it be patience, greater ability to listen, a sense of compassion for the person speaking? What passages are offered in the bible for any of those alternatives? For that day of contemplative prayer, select the one that shimmers for you and use it as a mantra. Sit in silence, describe your experience, and for your intention name a person or situation to whom you would like to respond rather than react. Live out your day performing the action as intended and, while you are doing it, note any sense of empowerment or insight from the grace of your morning's prayer. This seems to be an excellent way to begin with the end in mind and turn to scripture and presence to assist you in being intentional about transforming your relationship. This manner of proceeding lends itself to the analogy we used regarding driving a car by using what we see through the windshield to guide us, rather than trying to drive using the rear view mirror and looking what is now the past.

---

[101] Michael Brown, The Presence Process, pp. 244-249.

Sources for a Shimmering Phrase

There is no end to the sources you might have from which to draw shimmering phrases to reduce to one or two sacred words or mantras. They might include Psalms or biblical passages, poems, thoughts from spiritual reading, daily meditations books, or simply words or phrases that come to you spontaneously.

Contemplation and *Social* Action

It is true, contemplation will not only have an impact on your relationships, it will also impact your engagement in social and political action. It has to. When you have become one with the presence and have had your deepest longing for union fulfilled, the realization of that good will be diffusive of itself. Any true good we possess has that same inner dynamism. It moves from what is processed to what must be shared. We simply feel a compulsion to tell someone when a good comes to us. If that "good" is a oneness with all creation, a oneness that no longer is limited by my ego and own self-interest, if it is a union that sees everyone as a brother or sister, the protective walls that surround us are dismantled, and our presence quickens and supports us in moving out in risk, love, and forgiveness to our neighbor, particularly the one we may have previously labeled as enemy. Deep prayer that enters the unconscious will change the way you see the world. Rather than your adversary, the world becomes very much a part of you. From fleeing it, you will embrace it. The fragile self is gone. Contemplation moves you from ego-centered or world-centered. Your repeated presence to God allows God to work through you, empower you, and draw you forth into new areas and new levels of action and especially *social* action.

Who will the "you" be in such action? Rohr responds: *"It will be 'no longer you' who acts or contemplates, but the Life of One who lives in you*

(*Galatians 2:20*), *now acting for you (Father) and with you (Holy Spirit) and as you (Christ)!"*[102] And we do not have to wait for such social action to come to pass. If it is desirable to have that outlook now, begin with this end in mind, as the previous section stated. Take a passage from scripture such as Micah 6:8, *"He has shown you, O mortal, what is good. And what does the LORD require of you? To act justly and to love mercy and to walk humbly with your God,"* reduce it to a mantra of, say, *"justice and mercy,"* take it into the silence, describe the experience, state an intention as an attitude, and see what the Lord presents to you regarding an act of social action.

I find that *"beginning with the end in mind"* regarding social action is a helpful way to proceed, since it is an area in which I want to be more responsive to God's grace. The joy that may well follow is realizing that in your action, it is no longer you acting, but the one who lives within you, manifesting himself through you. Let Rohr conclude: *"Henceforth, it does not even matter whether you act or contemplate, contemplate or act, because both will be inside the One Flow, which is still and forever loving and healing the world."*[103]

Achieving a Way to "Pray always"

A few thoughts on the scriptural invitation to *"Pray always."* Scripture espouses the value of such a state of praying always:

> ➤ *"Look to the LORD and his strength; seek his face always."* (1 Chronicles 16:11)
>
> ➤ *"Then Jesus told his disciples...that they should always pray and not give up."* (Luke 18:1)

---

[102] Richard Rohr, "Life as Participation", *Richard Rohr's Daily Meditation*, September 17, 2014, adapted from *Dancing Standing Still: Healing the World from a Place of Prayer*, 4-5, 13-14, 18.
[103] Ibid.

> ➤ *"But in every situation, by prayer and petition...present your requests to God."* (Philippians 4:6)
> ➤ *"Devote yourselves to prayer, being watchful and thankful."* (Colossians 4:2)
> ➤ *"Pray continually."* (1 Thessalonians 5:17)

Even the most cloistered of monks and nuns are not able to pray always if the prayer that was being espoused was time spent in any of the three forms of prayer we have considered. Of course, a major portion of their day is indeed spent in formal prayer, but what is one to do with raising a family, working at a job, having a social life, and praying always? Again, we can look at a monastery and see that community welfare, tending to work, and social interaction are all provided for as well. It is then more a question of just how these acts are performed or what we bring to them that makes them prayerful. And so as mentioned before, our praying always is really comprised of formal prayer times when we dispose ourselves to meeting God on God's terms and coming out of that presence touched by God's grace. However, praying always is also comprised of God meeting us on our terms, which are the hundreds of everyday moments when community, work, or social interactions are taking place. It is true that our formal prayer may well contribute to the quality of how we shall be present, but even if this does not occur spontaneously, we can encounter any present moment of activity as a portal to go deeper, to suddenly see in it a blessing, a moment of grace. This means simply being present to the moment, as it is, with nothing added. What it takes is an openness to live that moment or any moment aware that there is more here than meets the eye. Thus the most menial of tasks contains a moment of revelation. *"What am I missing?"* or *"What do I notice?"* become important questions to help us break through and enter the portal of mystery and to delve into greater depths of awareness. The present moment, the activity "out there" in our daily lives becomes an extraordinary encounter with the divine. These two – formal prayer and the present moment – are the components of what it means to "pray always."

In order to live as "praying always," it takes more than one or two sessions a day to sit in silence and be so disposed to have God's presence experienced. It takes practice in both areas of formal prayer and being present to the present moment until they become habitual and second nature. Habit formation will be considered in chapter 5. When speaking of these two elements of "praying always," I have found it helpful to note them as IN→out activity, meaning we go "IN-to" the presence and come "out" with an experience and making an intention to put that grace into effect in the course of the day. The second element, relating to what is going on in any present moment, I would call OUT→in experiences. These are moments in the day that awareness allows us to see the presence of the divine and that a simple noticing and resting, with even just a single deep breath of appreciation, takes us deeper. Combining IN→out and OUT→in experiences creates the opportunity to experience *"praying always"* as the scriptures invite us to do.

The invitation to pray in and through the myriad of activities and occurrences that take place in one's day would suggest that not only does God care for us in those moments or that God can reveal himself to us in those moments, but that our longing for union is constantly expressing itself and that it can be fulfilled. God desires for us to have hearts that are receptive to transformation and with OUT→in noticings, our prayers are short and though *"small as mustard seeds,"*[104] posture us for unexpected and unimagined moments of transformation. For our part, it does take noticing something, stopping to let it sink in for a moment, reflecting on it briefly, and responding with a small thought of gratitude. Doing that a few times a day can make a big difference in how my day is experienced. When the thing "OUT there" happens to be an emotion welling up in us, such as stress on a difficult day, fatigue from a sleepless

---

[104] Matt. 17:20.

night, or weariness from the chores we are doing, these simple noticings make sense. In such moments of weakness, we might well realize that the Lord is our true strength. When we are tired, God will indeed sustain us. When we are caught up in endless worry, we can be reminded that we need to open our eyes to see how God is already working in our life in the moment and draw on his comfort. When we feel bitter or resentful, noticing, stopping, reflecting, and responding help us to recognize God's good gifts.

5

A SPIRITUALITY FOR DAILY LIVING

HOW BUSY DO WE NEED TO BE?

Look around and you can see it everywhere, especially among your friends and co-workers – busy, busy people. Everybody is busy, crazily busy. It has even become difficult to schedule social time with someone. It is akin to making an appointment long in advance. It gives us a sense of worth and value. It says we make a difference. Much of our busyness is self-imposed, as we take on more and more either at work or in our church or community, not to mention the on-line courses or working on the computer well into the night. In an article in *The New York Times* entitled *"The Busy Trap,"* Tim Kreider states that people are busy because of their own ambition or drive or anxiety because they're addicted to busyness and dread what they might have to face in its absence.[105]

This busyness hysteria has reached a fever pitch. Overwhelming as it may first seem, confronting it by taking five, then ten, then twenty minutes of prayerful sitting in silence each day is a first step. As you grow to enjoy this spaciousness that the divine presence fills so graciously, you want to begin to simplify your life; you want to unhook from the many things vying for your time and attention. You begin to realize

---

[105] Tim Kreider, "The 'Busy' Trap," *New York Times,* June 30, 2012, accessed November 15, 2015, http://opinionator.blogs.nytimes.com/2012/06/30/the-busy-trap/.

that busyness is not a necessary condition of life, but something we have chosen or something to which we have acquiesced. Kreider again, *"Busyness serves as a kind of existential reassurance, a hedge against emptiness; obviously your life cannot possibly be silly or trivial or meaningless if you are so busy, completely booked, in demand every hour of the day."*[106]

Committing myself to contemplative prayer over the years has slowed me down, so I am doing less, but doing it more deeply. This desire for slowing down began to get expressed in concrete actions in how I do things around the house or in my study. Every morning my in-box used to be full of e-mails asking me to do things I did not want to do or presenting me with problems that I had to solve, so I now use a junk email address I give whenever buying on-line, or someone I do not ever need to hear from again requests my address. I use the Google tabs so I never have to look at emails that automatically go into social, promotions, updates, or forums and instead just look at the primary tab. I never have my iPhone on ring, only on vibrate, and I do not answer calls when they come in, only an hour in the morning and an hour at the end of day. It has made some friends initially upset, but they have become accustomed to it. Friends, parishioners, and superiors now know that, and it has not created any problems in relationships. I have not watched a TV program or read a newspaper in seven years. My news comes as the day's top 10 headlines on the computer screen. In selecting movies at the theater or from Netflix, the friends I view them with are inclined, at my initiation, to select dramas over action movies. Such films are less violent, noisy, or in-your-face. When driving, audio books have replaced radio listening with its many ads, public service announcements, and egocentric personalities. Clearly, life has become less intolerable and more manageable. Remember, however, the satisfaction that comes from our longing for God becomes the steam that drives this engine of creating a less busy, less noisy, more reflective life.

---

[106] <u>Ibid</u>.

IN DEFENSE OF IDLENESS AND LEISURE

For most of us it takes a full week or two of vacation to decompress fully. Each increasing day away quiets us down and opens us up to a greater peace and serenity. Weekends, of course, are very different. They don't have the same ability to decompress, nor do they have the same spaciousness. There are social engagements, children's athletic games and activities, or doing the myriad of jobs that cry out for our attention. Narrow that down to a weekday, and there is even less of a sense of idleness or leisure. Going from the vacation week to the weekend to the weekday only raises the demand for my time and energy. Leisure doesn't have a chance and yet, it is when leisure is most needed. It is needed as a way of clearing my head, taking a breather, having a mental space where the subconscious can be making connections that otherwise would never take place. And if in that space there is no thinking but simple awareness, we are turning ourselves over to another source of presence and inspiration, another source of energy and wholeness. Daily prayerful leisure is not an indulgence or a vice. It is not a sign of wasting time. On the contrary, it may be some of the most important empowering time for the activities of the day. Idleness and leisure are as indispensable to the brain as vitamin D is to the body, and deprived of them, we could suffer a mental affliction as disfiguring as rickets. The space and quiet that idleness provides is a necessary condition for standing back from life in order to see it as a whole, for making unexpected connections, and for waiting for the wild summer lightning strikes of inspiration. It is, paradoxically, necessary to getting any quality work accomplished. History is replete with stories of inspirations that came in idle moments, that is, from a resting brain. Thomas Pynchon in an essay on sloth wrote, *"Idle dreaming is often of the essence of what we do."*[107]

---

[107] Thomas Pynchon, "The Deadly Sins/Sloth: Nearer, My Couch, to Thee," *New York Times Review*, June 6, 1993, accessed November 15, 2015, https://www.nytimes.com/books/97/05/18/reviews/pynchon-sloth.html.

GOOD MODELING PAST AND PRESENT

When reading the desert fathers and mothers, their descriptions of the states of contemplation are wonderfully expressive, and their individual methods for disposing themselves for those states are very helpful. As you read them, you may be inclined to say that the means of achieving those states are at best naive, at worst irrational. It helps to situate them in the culture of their time and the people within that culture to whom they were speaking. That can make a big difference. Union with the divine, disposing oneself to the presence, and having ways to maximize the quality of the time spent in the presence remain the same today as they were then. However, what I have noticed is that moving from the presence to action that makes a difference, and then tracking those actions as a way of discerning how God is influencing my life, has not been widely covered in the limited reading I have done on the subject. It is to fill that void that this book is written. A second point is worth noting. Twelve-step programs for addictions of all sorts have flourished in recent decades, and their formats hold a key to understanding how addictions can be overcome. It is not by shaming, reprimanding or telling the addict what he/she needs to do. Harmful substances are habit forming because they fulfill a need for intimacy, self-worth or connectedness. When those values are present in one's environment, the need for the substance is reduced. A recent TED Talk[108] on Addiction makes the point so well, *"The opposite of addiction is not sobriety; the opposite of addiction is connection."* [109] We have attempted to offer the greatest connection this side of heaven and to support the individual seeker in operationalizing the presence and

---

[108] **TED** is a nonprofit devoted to spreading ideas, usually in the form of short, powerful talks of 18 minutes or less. **TED** began in 1984 as a conference where Technology, Entertainment and Design converged, and today covers almost all topics — from science to business to global issues — in more than 100 languages.
[109] Johann Hari, "Everything you think you know about addiction is wrong." *Ted Talks,* https://www.ted.com/talks/johann_hari_everything_you_think_you_know_about_addiction_is_wrong, (November 17, 2015).

out of those repeated encounters expressed in action to discern God's plan for oneself. This final chapter, like the 12-step programs, pays close attention to daily routines for living in a connected fashion, development of individual and group relationships, where to get ongoing support, and monthly and annual continuing formation.

WHAT IS SPIRITUALITY?

A person's spirituality is the application of their religious beliefs and practices to their daily life and choices. It is the soulful consciousness with which they live in the moment. Their experience of the divine presence and their living out of this presence are consistent. Whether they are in deep contemplative presence or acting in the moment, the two realms not only appear as one, but are in fact one. When the individual is not consciously in the moment, their simplest of choices are more likely to be in harmony with their experience of divine presence, as the transcendent increasingly becomes their world view. When busyness is slowed down, when time is made for silence and leisure, the secrets of the mystics are revealed to the simplest of souls.

In *"The Inner Experience, Notes on Contemplation,"* Thomas Merton praises a life of contemplation and action and how the two meet in the present moment in which one is engaged:

> *The life of contemplation in action and purity of heart is, then, a life of great simplicity and inner liberty. One is not seeking anything special or demanding any particular satisfaction. One is content with what is. One does what is to be done, and the more concrete it is, the better. One is not worried about the results of what is done. One is content to have good motives and not too anxious about making mistakes. In this way one can swim with the living stream of life and remain at every moment*

in contact with God, in the hiddenness and ordinariness of the present moment with its obvious task.

At such times, walking down a street, sweeping a floor, washing dishes, hoeing beans, reading a book, taking a stroll in the woods — all can be enriched with contemplation and with the obscure sense of the presence of God. This contemplation is all the more pure in that one does not 'look' to see if it is there. Such 'walking with God' is one of the simplest and most secure ways of living a life of prayer, and one of the safest. It never attracts anybody's attention, least of all the attention of him who lives it. And he soon learns not to want to see anything special in himself. This is the price of his liberty.

The life of contemplation in action and purity of heart is a life of great simplicity. One is content to remain at every moment in contact with God, in the hiddenness and ordinariness of the present moment with its obvious task. At such times, walking down a street, sweeping a floor, washing dishes, hoeing beans, reading a book, taking a stroll in the woods – all can be enriched with contemplation and with the obscure sense of God's presence. This contemplation is all the more pure in that one does not 'look' to see if it is there. Such 'walking with God' is one of the simplest and most secure ways of living a life of prayer.[110]

Merton in this lengthy quote speaks of one who is able to pray always. Such a person's daily living is fed from his or her time in contemplative prayer that flowers in action and from an on-going awareness that the divine awaits him or her in every action of the day; all it takes is

---

[110] Thomas Merton, *The Inner Experience: Notes on Contemplation*, (New York: HarperCollins Publishers, 2003).

thoughtful presence, mindful breathing, or simple noticing. We have spoken of "IN→out" as expressing going IN-to the presence and taking the grace received out into our world. We also spoke of "OUT→in" as experiencing out there in the mundane and ordinary actions of our day a touch of awareness that took us OUT→in to the presence. Merton and sacred scripture assure us that it is a most effective way to *"Pray always."* Let us now turn to developing a spirituality of our very own.

How Prayer and Intentions Impact Spirituality

Tracking for a month can lead to discernment; discernment over several months can deepen intentionality, that is, intentions made each day. Intentionality leads to greater transformation through the grace of presence made explicit in the doing that takes place each day. Transformations create new ways to be in the world. It dispels the illusion that we are individual parts rather than individuations of the greater whole. As we reflect on the changes taking place, they may, in discussions with a spiritual director or spiritual guide, become explicit as an articulated spirituality that has slowly taken form over the past months.

Determining a Spirituality for Your Lifestyle or Changing Your Lifestyle to Suit Your Spirituality

One would think that you could come at spirituality one of two ways. It could be a style or way of acting that you would like to see or it could be an eventuality that you had not specifically intended, but are very pleased to discover that you have acquired. The means of coming at it either way are now at your disposal, either through daily intentions made as you come out of contemplative presence or reflection on your past month's prayer life to see the quality of your way of being with God and with others. Your friends and acquaintances would be very helpful in articulating any changes they may have noted. Whichever your starting point, contemplative prayer time will be an important element of the process. This will demand developing a habit for such daily prayer time. It is said that forming a habit can take anywhere from 21 to 67 days, depending on its difficulty. We will consider habit formation later in this chapter.

St. Paul as a Contemplative Practitioner

In his Letter to the Philippians, Paul reveals his secret for being a contemplative practitioner. Recall that while in prison, he is suffering many trials and describes himself as being in chains. Yet, for all the pain of imprisonment, his letter is filled with light, hope, and enthusiasm. A sound prayer life will reap those effects. Paul addresses the mind and specifically how to work with it. He has been able to tame an angry and combative mind, so God's grace of presence might have its effects on him. For some reason, that lesson has not been learned over the centuries of Christians that followed Paul. In his study of Philippians 4:7, *"Pray with gratitude, and the peace of God which is beyond all knowledge, will guard your hearts and your minds in Christ Jesus,"* Richard Rohr summarizes Paul's teaching regarding the use of the mind in contemplative prayer,[111] which I have rephrased in part as follows:

> ➤ First, begin positively, that is, with gratitude
> ➤ Second, one must get to a place beyond agitation, where there is peace, no matter how long it takes

---

[111] Richard Rohr, *In the Footsteps of St. Paul*, Audio CD, (Cincinnati: Franciscan Media, 2015)

➢ Third, Paul says that this place is a place beyond *"knowledge,"* that is, beyond the processing of information or ideas

➢ Fourth, learn how to stand guard. This standing guard is the witness we have developed above. It is the deeper you that can watch as a bystander what it going on in your mind, in both the flow of thoughts and the feelings on your heart

➢ Finally, be aware of your goal. Rohr writes, *"Your egoic thoughts can actually be replaced with living inside the very mind of Christ (en Cristo). This is not self-generated knowing, but knowing by participation--consciousness itself."* (con-scire, to know with)

It is quite stunning how Paul can put into one verse of scripture the entire process for transformation that we have been considering.

We now turn to environment, exercises, and resources that can maximize the quality of time spent in the presence by sharpening our intentions or increasing the quality of our paying attention in the moment. The present moment thus becomes a portal for deeper communion.

A Supportive Environment for Prayer

A Time and Place to Pray

We began this chapter with how busy we all are. In such a state, one will never find the time to pray unless one *"makes"* the time to pray. The Catechism of the Catholic Church is clear on this matter:

> The choice of the time and duration of the prayer arises from a determined will, revealing the secrets of the heart. One does not undertake contemplative prayer only when one has the time: one makes time for the Lord, with the firm determination not to give up, no matter what trials and dryness one may encounter.

One cannot always meditate, but one can always enter into inner prayer, independently of the conditions of health, work, or emotional state. The heart is the place of this quest and encounter, in poverty and in faith.[112]

Here we are thinking about a regular schedule that is easy to follow and does not get co-opted by a work schedule, a day off, a weekend, or even time away on a vacation. Because we have made the time for 20 to 30 minutes of silence, we are more likely to honor it as we honor our other commitments for which we have made time. Just like eating, while we eat in many different formats, such as taking lunch from home, securing fast food on the go, coming home to supper, dining in a restaurant, etc., we always make time to eat. By a spiritual life, we mean a concern for things of the Spirit and creating special times for attending to this. Making time for repeated actions, if they pay off, will create a craving in us to repeat them until a habit is formed. By a spiritual life, we mean a style of living that is grounded in a daily presence to God and a living out of that presence. The *"grounding and living out of"* can, if performed repeatedly, become habitual, but it will take a dedicated time, place, and format to facilitate its becoming so. We will consider habit formation in chapter 5.

It is important to develop a time of day that you are most open to sitting still. In the beginning, it need only be 10 minutes, but it must be a dedicated time and the same time each day under all conditions already mentioned. Mornings tend to be better times than evening or nighttime. It is for this reason that even in monastic schedules, just before dawn and early morning are the favored times in monasteries for long or repeated stretches of prayer. So, think about setting the alarm 15 minutes earlier and most importantly, think about having to retire 15 minutes earlier. When doing this for myself, I decided that I needed adequate time for spiritual reading, praying the Liturgy of the Hours, and sitting in silence.

---

[112] *Catechism of the Catholic Church*, 2710.

As a result, I set my wake-up time and then set a new retiring time. I gently informed many of my need to go to bed earlier: friends with whom I was vacationing, individuals with whom I was meeting at the parish, and families that I was visiting. At times, I would even ask for support in this. That was many years ago, and the parting from the groups for an earlier bedtime has not caused any problems, as folks have become used to the habit. There is also something very familiar that in whatever setting I find myself - home, hotel, rectory, on land, in the air, or on the water - my being in a space of prayer and reflection is so familiar, so comforting, and most important of all, supportive of my continuing to practice the habit.

After making available a time of day, sacred space is very important. One makes the space sacred by dedicating it for the special purpose of being present to God. Any space can offer us some aspect of the sacred. It may be nature as seen through a window or in a potted plant on a coffee table, the scent of a candle, the coziness of a room or a wrap laid across the sofa, an icon, a piece of sculpture, a painting or other work of art, or rosary beads laid on an end table. It is good to have a chair to sit in that is both comfortable and yet supportive of your spine, a chair in which you can sit straight, yet relaxed. Most importantly, the area should be free of distractions and noise. This quality of the space may impact the time of day one prays, causing you perhaps to rise a half hour earlier before others in the house stir. Some find that having a freshly brewed cup of coffee or tea present is a great way to wake up to the presence through aroma and taste. In such a case, the drink need not be a distraction for awareness and the presence, but a delightful preparation for it, knowing that its qualities will be reflected in the Divine Presence as a similar soothing warmth or a nourishing companion. With time, place, and environment established, you can begin to create a routine that supports letting go of worldly concerns and moving into pure awareness. If my mind is cluttered with several things I need to do in the course of the day, it is helpful simply to jot them down on a small spiral bound note pad to attend to after prayer time. With such items out of the way, a daily reading of a spiritual nature, as in a book of daily reflections or a daily email reflection from one of many spiritual sites, helps settle the mind. We will discuss this shortly. Others find one of the scripture readings assigned to the day helpful. For still others, sipping a cup of coffee brings about an inner peace. My routine is generally to jot down *"To Do"* items as a way of quieting my mind, sip a cup of coffee, read a daily meditation, note the readings for the Mass of the day, and from these sources seeing what phrase bubbles to the surface that speaks to me as I face the coming day. As different routines are tried, whichever gets me to a quiet state of awareness is the one I begin to crave as the best preparation for prayer and presence to the Lord.

Always at my disposal for going into the silence and coming out of it are the 4-step model of contemplative prayer and the 2-sided coin for contemplative action - two easy ways to experience God's presence and our movement from grace into action for our daily living.

Two Essential Apps

Once you have a setting and made time in your day, two apps for your smartphone can serve as powerful resources to disposing yourself to prayerful presence. One is *Insight Timer* at www.insighttimer.com and the other *Divine Office* at www.divineoffice.org. Both are means to quiet your mind and when added to breathing, they become powerful tools. *Insight Timer* offers you seven beautiful Tibetan singing bowl sounds that gently dispose you to the silence and beyond. The tones range from bright and clean to deep and complex with lovely overtones. There is also a wooden block that I use at the 15-minute interval as a gentle reminder to move to awareness in case I have been sidetracked by thinking and have gone off into a planning mode. The app allows you to time your session without worrying if you are running over. It allows for simple or advanced routines with interval bells, and when your session is over you are able to text in your mantra a word or two describing of the experience and stating your intention for the day. At the end of the month, if you would like a hard copy of your tracking for the purpose of discerning what has taken place over time, you simply export a month's journal entries via an email attachment. Journal access may be password protected to ensure privacy. There is an excellent statistics feature that helps you track your progress over time on how your practice is evolving.

An additional important feature is the opportunity that *Insight Timer* gives you to be part of a global contemplative community. You are able to see easily who is praying anywhere throughout the world in real time. It is easy to find folks in your own city of postal area code who are sharing your spiritual journey and friend them on Facebook. If you wish, you could see who might be interested in gathering for a monthly session in the same physical space. The opportunities are endless!

A second app that I use everyday in my prayer is *Divine Office,* and it was voted best Catholic iPhone and iPad App over several years. It affords you the opportunity to participate in the recitation of the Liturgy of the Hours, which is the public prayer of the Christian community. The *"Office,"* as it is called by many, is an ancient collection of psalms, hymns, and readings from scripture. The hymns are sung by wonderful choirs; the four readers will sing parts of the Office and chant the Psalms on Sundays and feast days. If you are unable to pray in the company of others, there is a feature that makes it possible to view locations of others who are praying with you in real time. There are seven such times to pray each day. Each is called *"an hour"* but many take 10 to 20 minutes. Most will pray Morning Prayer and Night Prayer. It is a wonderful way to pray with others and maintain an intimate connection with God. If we are to take St. Paul seriously when he advises the Christians at Thessalonica and us (5:17) to *"pray without ceasing,"* he is talking of all three forms of prayer and also being attentive to what we are doing in the present moment, as God may reveal himself. Praying the *Divine Office* maximizes the quality of our verbal/vocal prayer, even when alone and prayed in solidarity with a world wide community.

CREATING A LIST OF APHORISMS

Aphorisms are those pithy observations containing a general truth that were initially put in our heads as children by our parents and teachers. *"When you've got your health you have everything," "Be grateful for the things you have,"* and *"You can bring a horse to water, but you can't make him drink"* are part of the list that was etched into the childhood brains in our family. As one who now espouses contemplative presence, it is good to create an ongoing list of such pithy statements that get to the heart of the matter for you when it comes to the longing you have for God. A few of mine from a much longer list follow:

> ➢ *"If we have abandoned ourselves to God, there is only one rule for us: the duty of the present moment."* Jean-Pierre de Caussade
> ➢ *"Pray always as a stance in your world you are present to the Presence and present to that same Presence in all things."* Richard Rohr
> ➢ *"This is what it means to be awake: to be constantly willing to say that God could even be coming to me in this! Even in this! Just this!"* Eckhart Tolle
> ➢ *"If you are to experience the ever-present and ever-coming Christ, the one place you have to be is the one place you are usually not: NOW HERE or "nowhere."* Richard Rohr
> ➢ *"Once we change the nature of our relationship with each moment to that of an awakened stance, formlessness can function through form, and spirit can shine through our transformed, utterly unique self."* Kathleen Dowling Singh

SEVEN WAYS TO EXPERIENCE CONTEMPLATION ONLINE

The Internet is a wonderful cornucopia of contemplative resources. The following list of seven suggestions may prove helpful for you:

➢ **Quiet Music:** Find a station on *Pandora, iTunes,* or your favorite streaming music site, and listen to something that brings you into a contemplative space. In this regard yoga, relaxation, or ambient radio channels on Pandora could be helpful.

➢ **Prayer Website:** *Sacred Space,* a favorite of mine. It has been maintained by the Irish Jesuits of Dublin since 1999. You are invited into a quiet, prayerful space online and led through meditative prayer, ending with a scripture passage with which to sit.

➢ **Liturgy of the Hours:** This app was covered earlier in this chapter.

➢ **Meditation Timer:** This app also was covered above. For those who want more than just a timer or link to community, the app provides guided meditations by Thich Nhat Hanh, Tara Brach, Jack Kornfield, and Eckhart Tolle among others.

➢ **An Online Course:** There is a proliferation of courses, classes, and webinars offered online for credit, continuing education, and personal nourishment. Abbey of the Arts offers an eight day *Monk in the World e-Course,* and Contemplative Journal offers an e-Course on *Aging as a Spiritual Practice.* The Shalem Institute has new offerings regularly.

➢ **Articles and Blog Postings:** As I am working on the Internet, I will often run across an interesting article to add to my list of *"evening entertainment"* or it may be something I go to right now to break for a brief moment the monotony of a project on which I am working. I find such nuggets of contemplative information are just what the doctor ordered to get my mind in a different groove for a while. I regularly reread Richard Rohr's *Daily Meditations* and Thomas Keating's meditations on *Contemplative Outreach.* They are often like a whiff of pure oxygen when the air I've been breathing has become stale.

➢ **Social Media:** A final suggestion would be to find contemplative organizations and individuals you enjoy and to follow them on social media. It is a good way to connect with resources and people who have the same passion for presence. I belong to a contemplative aging group that reads a chapter of a book each month and shares reflections via an email thread. We are just completing Ilia Delio's *"The Unbearable Wholeness of Being."* Our new book is *Sacred Fire: A Vision for a Deeper Human and Christian Maturity* by Ronald Rolheiser. Most of the groups mentioned above can be connected to using FaceBook.

These are seven suggestions that have fed me on my spiritual journey and continue to do so each day. Whether I want a spiritual calm from gazing at a contemplative photo or relishing an insightful quote, whether I want to spend a meaningful half-hour on a pertinent article or I'm ready to explore contemplative practice in greater depth, a myriad of choices are just a mouse click away. And this is a *"bank account"* that only continues to build.

Other Exercises

Spending a Few Moments in Gratitude Each Evening

A very worthwhile practice to begin at bedtime is simply to list five things in the course of the day for which you are grateful. They need not be earthshaking events, but simple things you noticed that came your way. If you make it a rule not to repeat any one of the blessings ever, you will begin to experience more and more things you would not have noticed before. After all, not being able to repeat any makes you have to search more deeply.

A second benefit accrues from such a gentle nightly habit. You will begin to experience blessings as they take place rather than simply in the recollection of them. I am reminded of how many photos we take, now with the availability of smartphones, the vacation is experienced more in the recollection than in the joy of the present moment. Perhaps we need to put down the camera and enjoy and savor the moment for it will never return with the same intensity and presence. I do this increasingly as I prepare to shoot and ask myself, *"But isn't savoring this moment what I need to do rather than snapping a photo to enjoy later and quickly moving on to the next photo opportunity?"* I am taking a lot fewer photos and enjoying the moment more.

Slowly the tangible and measurable evidence that the power of gratitude can bring to the physical, financial, relational, mental, emotional, and/or spiritual aspects of your life will reveal themselves. Gradually, you will come to understand more fully the wisdom of Jesus when he said, *"For whoever has will be given more, and they will have an abundance. Whoever does not have, even what they have will be taken from them."*[113] A little practice of gratitude each evening becomes a powerful way to enhance your day.

THE IGNATIAN EXAMEN

An exercise that many find helpful in supporting their contemplative lifestyle is the daily use of the Ignatian Examen. The easiest way to get into the 10-minute before bedtime practice is simply to begin thinking of the things for which you are grateful, as explained above, since gratitude is one of the steps in the Examen. In short, the Examen has the five following parts posed as questions on which to reflect briefly. Gallagher's presentation and renaming each of the steps as Gratitude, Petition, Review, Forgiveness and Renewal have given the standard titles a fresh contemporary ring:[114]

---

[113] Matt. 25:29.

[114] Timothy M. Gallagher, OMV, *The Examen Prayer*, (Spring Valley: The Crossroad Publishing Company, 2006), 57ff.

1. *Thanksgiving/Gratitude*

   - *Lord, I realize that all, even myself, is a gift from you.*

   - *Today, for what things am I most grateful? (Rest in the gratitude)*

   - *Here we simply call forth gratitude for the blessings and gifts of the day, recognizing that they are the means through which God pours forth his love for me.*[115] *Acknowledging these gifts is the surest way to love God in return and to experience the relationship we have.*

2. *Intention/Petition*

   - *Lord, open my eyes and ears to be more honest with myself.*

   - *Today, what do I really want for myself?*

   - *Here we are asking the Lord what he wants to show us about the day, to make connections or have insights regarding what took place. Ignatius says that in this step desire, now warmed by gratitude, takes shape as a petition of the heart, asking that grace effect in us what God has inspired us to "wish and desire"*[116] *The grace asked for is both the gift of understanding and deeper insight into how God is working in our day. In this way we can have a greater impact in our relationship with God.*

3. *Examination/Review*

   - *Lord, show me what has been happening to me and in me this day.*

   - *Today, in what ways have I experienced your love?*

   - *The day is then reviewed either by period of even hour by hour to see how events unfolded and may have been connected. There will be moments of consolation as well as desolation. How were each responded to? Considering the day and its events, you now look to conforming your heart to God's.*

---

[115] St. Ignatius of Loyola, *The Spiritual Exercises of Saint Ignatius*, #234, (New York: DoubleDay, 1964).

[116] St. Ignatius of Loyola, *The Spiritual Exercises of Saint Ignatius* #48, (New York: DoubleDay, 1964).

4. *Contrition/Forgiveness*

- *Lord, I am still learning to grow in your love.*
- *Today, what choices have been inadequate responses to your love?*
- *Knowing that God loves us as we are, warts and all, we become keenly aware that God loves others in precisely the same way. This empowers us to love ourselves and them as God loves. The marvel of the Examen is that we can experience deeply this love. It is borne of simply being attentive to and noticing this outpouring of love. Gratitude disposes our hearts to receive this forgiveness. We are able to look at our faults for what they are in peace and to trust in God's merciful love.*

5. *Hope/Renewal*

- *Lord, let me look with longing toward the future.*
- *Today, how will I let you lead me to (forgiving another) (a brighter tomorrow)?*[117]

The action of looking back in the first four steps (Today, for what things am I most grateful? / Today, what do I really want for myself? / Today, in what ways have I experienced your love? / Today, what choices have been inadequate responses to your love?) is only to prepare ourselves for looking forward in the fifth. Recognizing my faults in 1-4, I can better understand what God wants of me and make amends in step 5, choose a path to greater spiritual growth, no matter what the temptation that lies before me. The intention that is the Renewal step becomes the cutting edge of transformation for the next day. Thus, we learn each day from the prior day's experience, which becomes an extraordinary resource for our spiritual transformation. It is worthwhile to note that the *examen* can serve to enhance our understanding in tracking the intentions made after contemplative prayer and how those intentions were actualized.

---

[117] Adapted from *Through All the Days of Life*, a collection of prayers compiled by Fr. Nick Schiro, S.J.

HUMAN RESOURCES

SPIRITUAL DIRECTORS OR SPIRITUAL GUIDES

Apart from the daily routines that can become life-giving habits for prayer and presence, there are contacts with others who share the same value for silence and interaction with others. Part of the great success of 12-step groups is their ability to have a sponsor and a place to regularly share what is going on with them with others. For this reason, it is strongly advised that one who prays regularly also seek a spiritual guide, companion, or director with whom to meet regularly. Generally, such meetings take place every four to six weeks and go for an hour.

At each meeting, the individuals can share how things are going with regard to their prayer and their relationship with God. Of special significance would be to note surprises that arose since the last meeting, as well as any resistances he or she has experienced. Surprises and resistances are ground for very fruitful insights. Regarding such surprises, as these are noted, it helps one refine the eyes with which they see and are thus able to see, more deeply into the simple, gentle, ordinary events of the day, God's special presence. Resistances are emotional expressions that are deeply felt. What is of special interest is what the resistance is about. *Why or what am I resisting?* To delve into such questions is to clear the way for what is trying to break through by way of God's initiative, and as they are noted and acknowledged for what they truly are, the path for grace to flow more abundantly is opened.

Spiritual guides are there for the finding. Good sources for names would be your pastor, spiritual friends, or members of your church, or simply Google *"Catholic or Christian Spiritual Directors"* along with your postal area code to find resources in your area. Another way would be to contact the Shalem Institute in Washington, DC and ask for graduates of their Spiritual Guidance Program who live in your area. Finally, location need not be a hindrance. Many individuals have a director or guide in a faraway state and have their monthly direction via Skype or FaceTime. If it is a wider community or grouping you are looking for with which to share contemplative prayer and contemplative issues, they are easy to find on the Internet, and another good source is right on your *Insight Timer* app, where you can select other individuals who are in contemplative prayer even in your location and inquire from several if there is any interest in coming together once a month for prayer together. The avenues for connecting and experiencing spiritual community are limitless.

PRAYER PARTNERS

Very often after retreatants have been together for a weekend or week, bonds have begun to form and a sense of spiritual community has begun. In many cases, individuals will begin exchanging email addresses or requesting a sign-up list for any who would like to stay in touch as a group. It is at such times that I encourage individuals who have begun a relationship to become prayer partners and at regular intervals (weekly, bi-weekly or monthly) to email each other with a request for prayer. It is an excellent way to remain connected. A very powerful way to pray for and with someone is to take their intention, e.g., to face the results of a lab test with calm or to overcome a lingering habit, and to sit in silence a few moments breathing deeply. After a while to say, for example as you breathe in, *"Sally or Bill, I take in your anxiety for the test results"* and on the out breath say something like, *"I shower you with peace."* The important thing is that the inhale is an expression of your solidarity with the person's pain, struggle, or concern, and the exhale is both your prayer request and participation in the person's empowerment. This form of intercessory prayer puts your request at the feet of the Lord, has you take some of the pain to yourself, and bonds you with the one for whom you are praying. In addition to specific prayer requests exchanged between prayer partners, a good way to keep the relationship focused on contemplative prayer and action, as it applies to your new lifestyle, is to ask each time:

> ➤ *"How's it going with God this week?"*
> ➤ *"What surprises did you discover?"*
> ➤ *"What resistances are you in touch with?"*

While they are easy questions, their answers will go a long way in seeing how God is interacting in your life and what is impeding the flow of grace.

Spiritual Community or Support of a Faith Community

As the yearning for God's presence grows, so too does the desire to be with others who are on a similar journey of union. Observing and celebrating the Sabbath is an important part of growth in what is happening in your contemplative prayer. *The Catechism of the Catholic Church* states it well when is says, *"Contemplative prayer is a union with the prayer of Christ insofar as it makes us participate in his mystery. The mystery of Christ is celebrated by the Church in the Eucharist, and the Holy Spirit makes it come alive in contemplative prayer so that our charity will manifest it in our acts."*[118]

In the Gospel of John, Jesus, as part of his final discourse, affirms the centrality of this prayer of union with him, our coming together, and sacred action,

> *My prayer is not for them alone. I pray also for those who will*
> *believe in me through their message, that all of them may be one,*
> *Father, just as you are in me and I am in you. May they also be*
> *in us so that the world may believe that you have sent me. I have*

---

[118] *Catechism of the Catholic Church*, 2718.

given them the glory that you gave me, that they may be one
as we are one — I in them and you in me — so that they may
be brought to complete unity. Then the world will know that
you sent me and have loved them even as you have loved me.[119]

What is critical here is the prayer for complete unity of those Jesus is leaving behind. And the unity is a vertical unity they have with Christ. Horizontally, they may not comprise the structural unity of being in the same church, the same denomination, or the same elements of doctrine, but each of the multitude is united to Christ in some direct way, thus the unity experienced across denominational lines is indeed possible. The oneness for which Jesus prays, therefore, may literally be that we are one in him, no matter what label of Christianity we wear. It is precisely this sense of spiritual community that is experienced as a small community of retreatants, or members of a diverse prayer group, or believers coming together for common prayer. The prayer, and particularly contemplative prayer, becomes a common feeding of the branches with the life-giving sap of the vine that is Christ that takes place. Let our presence to God as Father Creator, Son Redeemer, or Life-giving Spirit, then, be the tie that binds us into a spiritual community.

Spiritual Enrichment

Regular Day of Recollection, Annual Retreat, On-Line Spirituality Offerings

Daily prayer routines, monthly check-ins, and spiritual community are the bread-and-butter of a healthy and vibrant prayer life. A longer-range resource would be an annual retreat, either silent or directed. Many monasteries and

---

[119] John 17:20-23.

retreat houses offer individual silent retreats where you can simply go and be on your own in an environment that totally saturates you in space and awareness, being able to leave TV, smartphone, laptops, meal preparation, job and family behind for a weekend or week. Also offered are directed retreats, either individual or in a group setting. Even these will allow for lots of quiet time and reflection. Annual retreats are often looked at as akin to pulling into a filling station after your gas tank has run dry after a year and you are in need of filling up. Another way to think about a retreat would be to see it as a transformational time where new inputs and insights can cause a shift in consciousness into a new way to live your life, one grounded more in contemplative presence with daily intentions that make a difference in how your life is lived. With such a spiritual marker each year, one could note how this year's retreat made a difference in my living and in my relationship with God in comparison to last year's.

FORMING OF A DAILY HABIT OF PRAYER AND ACTION

I began this book with the longing each of us has for God, a longing placed within us by a creating, loving God who sent us forth in his own image that we might be fruitful and return to him in joy. That journey back is never a straight path. Even the mystics speak of the curves, potholes, bends, wrong turns, dead ends, peaks, and valleys to their coming home to God. Can we expect anything less? That said, it is important to recognize how much a part poor choices, bad decisions, and false starts play in our waking up to the fact that we need a guide, a trailblazer to help us on the journey. In Christ, we do have such a pioneer.

The journey forward in the spiritual life is really a journey inward, but where to find what you need for that inner journey? As one of the antiphons for the Office of Readings has it, *"Turn to God and he will give you everything you need."* For the one seeking contemplative prayer as a daily way to pray, the *"everything you need"* isn't so much the answer to prayers for specific requests, but more the grounding in God that then helps me to know God's will for me by the way he shares so abundantly his grace of presence with me. Praying this way is not so much a strengthening our *"love muscle"* so we can clench our teeth and give it our best shot in *"loving"* with an irksome fellow worker. It is much more a realization of how much God loves me and how closely I am joined to all people. With such a grace, such a perspective, we cannot help but be drawn to be more compassionate and loving, so we have the longing and the means to satisfy it. How, out of this, do we create a lifestyle that becomes habitual?

It appears that our goal in such a prayer life is more an active-contemplative lifestyle where what we do is shaped by our time spent in the presence, as well as the events and experiences of the day shaping our contemplative moments.

Regular time set aside for contemplative prayer and contemplative action can become a life-giving habit. The idea is that rather than decide, *"Should or do I have time today to pray?"* praying for that 20 to 30 minutes becomes as much a habit as does getting up, showering and dressing for the day's activities. Forty percent of the actions people perform each day are not actual decisions, but habits. Habits make for efficient, automatic responses to common everyday repeated needs. It is said that habits take 21 to 67 days to form or change. It stands to reason that the more stable and deeply rooted the habit, the longer it will take to change.

Make no mistake about it, a habit can be changed. It will be more possible to change if we understand how habits work. A habit is a group of choices that all of us deliberately made at some point and then stopped thinking about, but continued doing them - often every day. With the gaining of the habit, we were eventually able to stop making a choice, and the behavior becomes automatic.

In his best seller, *The Power of Habit* by Charles Duhigg, the author states that, *"It's a natural consequence of our neurology."*[120] Understanding

---

[120] Charles Duhigg, *The Power of Habit*, (New York: Random House Trade Paperbacks, 2012), 19.

how a habit takes place, one can rebuild those patterns in whichever way one chooses.

Duhigg speaks of the Habit Loop comprised of a cue, routine, and reward. See Figure #9: *"The Habit Loop."*

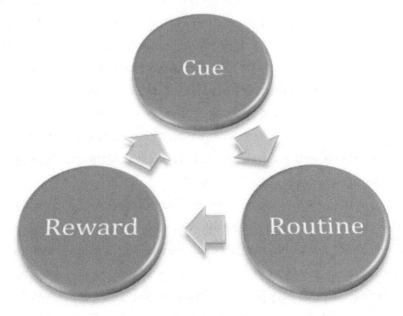

The Habit Loop

It is important to remember that habits never really disappear. Instead, they are encoded into the very structures of our brain and become automatic. Remember from our high school days Pavlov and his salivating dog! Given the loop, how does one go about changing a habit? Once a new habit, such as a daily 20-30 minute period of time each morning, is created to replace an older one of say, sleeping in or reading the newspaper, the new one can overrule the old one. From our own experience, we know that a habit can emerge without our permission. A case in point could be how a family or individual begins a *"fast-food"* eating habit.

Craving is the key to changing a habit. Once the routine creates a habit, once the brain anticipates the reward, other distractions lose their allure, and the anticipation and sense of craving become prominent. Yes, new habits, new routines, are so powerful that they create neurological cravings. We associate the cues with rewards, and the craving starts the habit loop over again. For example, if you were trying to lose ten pounds that you put on during vacation, just turning away from desserts or regulating portion size could be a mammoth task and one you might not be motivated to follow in the heat of a slice of cheesecake. However, if you are on the notch of the belt that makes it wider, and if your soul is the notch for the smaller size, that might be the motivation to turn down the dessert. Here, the *"craving"* for the smaller size belt notch created a greater motivation than the desire for the cake. We have to beware of dangerous cues and rewards, such as the smell of sugar and cinnamon filling the airline terminal from the Cinnabon food stall or the handy open 24-hours McDonalds. Cross the line once, it's easier to cross the line a second, third, and fourth time, and eventually, you have formed a habit you never thought you had! It is important that the desire for the reward create a craving. See Figure #10: *"The Craving Brain."*

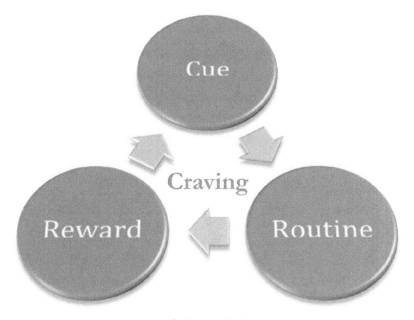

The Craving Brain

For us, the desire for union face-to-face with God will create the craving. It is for this reason that when reflecting on the experience of divine presence we repeatedly asked, *"How was the experience described different from other experiences described with the same word or words?"* The attempt is to show how much more satisfying, lasting, rarified, and unique such encounters with the face of God are and to create a craving for this depth and intensity that will motivate us to continue coming back for more, if you will, until the new habit is established. Yes, craving helps combat distractions; craving motivates; craving anticipates the reward of the new behavior and the reward. Habits once established will continue to create neurological cravings. From my own experience of gaining the habit of daily interval training or that of nutritious eating, both of which needed drastic improvement, I began to see my habits deepen as I moved from discomfort to comfort, from guilt to pride, from fear to self-possession, and from low self-esteem to greater self-esteem. The new habits formed became a gift to myself.

Forming a new habit loop is indeed possible and especially when it involves God's grace coming to us. We are reminded that as the nature grows, the grace flows. The converse is also true, that as the grace flows, the nature grows. What a marvelous symbiosis! Once again, as we saw with understanding habits, the new habit loop is driven by *"craving"* as a motivator. Duhigg lists the following steps for creating a new walking habit.[121]

1. *Plan a specific ROUTINE for your exercise*
2. *Create a CUE for the routine, e.g., sneakers, socks, shorts, headset out before going to bed*
3. *Create a CRAVING for the REWARD. Visualize it, hold it, have a photo of it*
4. *Let the craving drive the loop, help you with distractions, keep you motivated*

---

[121] Ibid., 51-52.

The following may be how one might create a new eating habit. We know that 78% of successful dieters eat breakfast. So for your 3 meals, you may eat breakfast like a king, lunch like a prince, and dinner like a pauper. Most of the successful dieters envisioned a specific reward for sticking to their plan, and when temptations arose, they focused on craving the reward. It is easy to move from these two applications to creating the daily habit of contemplative prayer. The routine is already established. The cue could be sacred music on your wake-up alarm, a prayer of dedication on your bathroom mirror, a cross on your wall, or it may be the lighting of a scented candle as you put on the coffee. The craving for the reward is easy: simply place a list of the words describing the experiences of a week's prayer sessions. You also have how each day the prayer experiences were more satisfying than experiences described with the same word or words. And thus, the cue gets you started and the craving moves you forward and, of course, God's grace, for a closer union of the lover and the beloved, is the silent depth of the ocean that floats the boat!

My own spirituality has been transformed significantly over the past ten years as old habits transformed into new ones. The years have seen me move from a change of ministry as a pastor of a parish with a Catholic School, to full-time contemplative ministry leading retreats, parish missions and days of recollection. In addition to new habits formed regarding two half-hour sessions of daily contemplative prayer, some old habits have gone by the wayside. While I am not necessarily advocating this for others, my life style has been shaped by a decided shift in spirituality. I live a life with much silence amid the Amish in southeastern Pennsylvania surrounded by woods, streams, and many forms of wildlife. I no longer drink spirits of any kind, watch TV, save coupons, or listen to the news. It is advertising and the noisy atmosphere of so much palaver of co-hosts and guests that no longer interests me. News now comes as headlines on a laptop, so I can be in touch with the world nationally and internationally to draw individuals and efforts into my prayer intentions and become the subject for prayer. The elements of a new lifestyle fueled by a spirituality of contemplative prayer and contemplative action are shared with a best friend in preparation for our Sunday homilies, with laity on my blog and other social networks, and at monthly gatherings of my clergy support group, parish contemplative prayer group, and contemplative listening circle. Clearly, a contemplative spirituality has become habitual.

CONCLUSION

EVERYTHING IS HOLY AND LESS IS MORE

Our mind and our senses working together have created a sense of separation between us and all objects, including ourselves. It is because knowing calls us to be at one and the same time, the subject knowing and the object known. This applies, as well, to ourselves and God. Thus, we spend our days actually craving to be one, yet using thinking as a means toward that end keeps us from the very goal we seek. Contemplation changes all that. Embracing the other, respecting and loving it, not trying to know it, becomes the present ground of all existence, and in the silence of the moment, we can achieve that sublime union. Kathleen Dowling Singh has said it succinctly,

> Relying upon only our senses and conceptual mind, we have
> created an experience of existence marked by separation:
> separation from others, from our own essential nature, and
> from the Sacred.... Love [is] the very presence of the Sacred....
> We spend much of our lives ignorant of the love in which we live
> and move and have our being.... We do not, in our ordinary,
> everyday minds, recognize love as our ever-present ground, our
> hallowed Reality. It is only through the eye of contemplation

that we can realize and come to know our essential nature and the essential, holy nature of all things.... With that revelation of Presence, we surrender what was always only an illusory ego and, no longer obstructed, enter the open arms of formless awareness....

"We come, gradually, with love's intention, to see that this form, this self we mistook for the final statement on our being, is here as function. Once we change the nature of our relationship with each moment to that of an awakened stance, formlessness can function through form and spirit can shine through our transformed, utterly unique self."[122]

There have been many lifestyle changes for me that stem from contemplative prayer that flowered in a spirituality. Based more on consolation, that is, what brought me greater joy or sense of well-being, a standard of measure that grew out of contemplative prayer, I simply moved in my choices toward a *"Less is more"* or a *"Don't get distracted by the glitter"* mentality. This is not to say that the choices were a flight from anything that was in itself bad or evil. They just no longer attracted me the way they used to. Several years ago, I decided that I wanted my smartphone to serve me at my request rather than have me available 24/7 for a majority of calls that were of no consequence. As a result, I made choices regarding the phone for a more contemplative and centered lifestyle. I no longer carry it around in my pocket. I do not take calls but only do callbacks and those at certain designated times of the day. Speaking of *"less is more,"* the maxim came alive in going through my small rancher. Cleaning out clothes closets; reducing all bookcases; cleaning out the basement, workshop, laundry, and garage; and not

---

[122] Kathleen Dowling Singh. "Full Circle: The Evidence of Love," in *Oneing:Evidence*, Vol. 2, No. 1 by Richard Rohr, (Albuquerque: Center for Action & Contemplation, 2014), 63-70.

bringing something into the house without taking something out to the dumpster so clutter never accumulates again have all radically changed the look of things at home. The rooms seem to be able to breathe again.

Jesus admonishes us to remain in love.[123] It is for Christians the great commandment. It is in contemplative prayer that awareness becomes the occasion for God's self-manifestation to us as mystical love. As our longing for God is fulfilled in such presence, we become in our actions and interactions the very love we experience. This empowers us not only to be instruments of love to others, but to see love and goodness where we had not seen it before. Abide in peace within, and we will see peace outside of ourselves. Abide in beauty within, and we will see beauty outside of ourselves. The experience of habitual contemplative prayer and of being able to remain in the present moment move religion from the esoteric realms of creedal statements and moral codes, where it has been for too long, into the lived experienced of believing. Living in such a way requires no moral codes beyond being an open and loving person both in mind and heart.

APPLICATION TO FAMILY LIFE, CAREER OR MINISTRY

While creating a daily life that is grounded in contemplation is a desirable goal, it cannot be achieved alone, nor can it be sustained by dogged determination. It is not easy to talk to family and those at work about your newfound craving for silence or having a love that encompasses all. It frankly is not easy to leave the presence of others to *"go off and pray."* People will either think you are strange, overly proud, or a bit asocial. It is for this reason that a first segment of silence should take place long before anyone in your life is stirring, including spouse, children, pets, or co-workers. If this time alone is sought in the evening, it becomes all the

---

[123] John 15:4-5.

more difficult to maintain, since you are normally more tired at the end of the day, and there is much commotion at work, at home, or in a social setting with friends. At home, if it is some silent time I desire, I am able simply to say, *"I need some quiet time,"* period. At work, if I want to spend half my lunch period slowly walking the grounds and people ask what I am doing, I simply say, *"I've promised myself a solitary half-hour walk each day to clear my head."* It seems to suffice. As pastor, I was able to combine four monthly meetings into two evenings, rather than spend four evenings a week meeting, by attending the beginning of one and the ending of the other. Also, any home I was invited to for dinner or when dining out with friends, at the time of the invitation I would make it clear what time I needed to leave to have some quiet time before retiring. In all cases, people understood, and, at times, it even came across as good modeling for them to do something along the same vein.

CLOSING THOUGHTS

As I was concluding this book, Christians around the world were experiencing the 12 days of Christmas. I was struck by how in Jesus becoming one of us, all things human become vehicles for a deeper union with both his human and divine natures. It is not just some mystical, far off God I contact in the silence, but all that is human in Jesus and in myself are the tangible touch points that help usher me into the divinity of Christ's presence. Sitting, breathing, using of a few words, the scent of a candle, the sound of a singing bowl – yes, even distractions and thoughts ¬ all can be bodily touch points to divine presence. Everything in creation and all feelings and emotions can speak to us. Everything in our created world has meaning. And then once there before the very presence, the very face of God, we are in God's hands. Back out of the silence, our reflection on what the experience was like brings the divine back into the human as I create an intention and live out of it. Reviewing these movements over weeks and months, I am able to note patterns and discern where God might be calling me, and my cooperating, which I hold loosely, is part of that emerging future. The human, the silence, and the future become three strands of life that are lived in God.

APPENDICES

APPENDIX

A

STEPPING STONES

(From: Kathleen Adams. *"Journal to the Self,"* Warner Books, p. 148)

"The Steppingstones are indicators that enable a person to recognize the deeper-than-conscious goals toward which the movement of his life is trying to take him." Dr. Ira Progoff. The following exercise is taken from *"Journal to the Self"* by Kathleen Adams.

When speaking of steppingstones in our prayer life, we mean those events that come to mind when we spontaneously reflect on the course that our life has taken in terms of prayer from our earliest consciousness to the present moment.

Like the steppingstones you choose carefully in crossing a turbulent stream, similarly steppingstones in your life of prayer are those moments where you became aware of prayer and took some ownership of a new way of thinking and relating to it. Thus your earliest steppingstone may have been your grandmother walking around the house with the silent words on her lips, or the candle that burned before you on the coffee table, a religious event in your life.

Steppingstones are neutral with respect to pleasure or pain, progress or failure. They are simply the markers that are significant to you as you reconstruct the movement of what would become your prayer life.

Let each steppingstone present itself as its own gift without comparison to the one before or the one after. Limit your selection to 12-15, for your intention is to select those events regarding your prayer life that seem to have significance within the context of how you are praying or not praying today. These will be the steppingstones of your prayer life, as you perceive it today. This is so, because the life events that affect your life as you are living it today will change as your life circumstances change.

Begin your list with the first steppingstone: *"I was born."* Your list can be written in random or chronological order. If it is written in random order, you can go back and renumber the items in chronological order.

1. _____
2. _____
3. _____
4. _____
5. _____
6. _____
7. _____
8. _____
9. _____
10. _____
11. _____
12. _____
13. _____
14. _____
15. _____

Reflective Work

Writing about the entire time frame allows you to recapture the events and moments that shaped your destiny. As you recall the time, you will find that lessons left incomplete are offered back up for learning; old wounds that never quite healed are offered back for healing.

Using the phrase, *"It was a time when…"* is the springboard from which you can enter each of the steppingstone periods. For example, regarding the stepping stone *"Returning from a family member's baptism"* could be: *"It was a time when … I felt moved, realizing that I too had been baptized many years ago and that I was called to live a life in intimate union with Christ."*

As you reflect on the metaphor or emotion that completes each phrase,

"It was a time when…" allow yourself to turn, not only your thoughts, but also your feelings, your body, and your soul to that period of your life. You may experience a rush of memories, images, associations, smells or tastes. Savor the rush! Let it wash over you and when you are ready in silence and solitude, begin to write in the first person about the steppingstone period.

B

BREATHING TECHNIQUES

(From: *6 Breathing Exercises to Relax in 10 Minutes or Less*
Jordan Shakeshaft, www.greatist.com, September 15, 2015)

Overworked, underslept and feeling the pressure? There are plenty of ways to find calm, without investing in a four-hand spa massage. All you need is a pair of lungs, your breath and 10 minutes or less. Don't wait until fight or flight kicks in before minding your breath. Controlled breathing not only keeps the mind and body functioning at their best, it can also lower blood pressure, promote feelings of calm and relaxation and help us de-stress. While the effects of breathing techniques on anxiety haven't yet been studied at length (at least not in a controlled clinical setting), many experts encourage using the breath as a means of increasing awareness, mindfulness or, for the yogis among us, finding that elusive state of Zen. To get to the bottom of the breath work, Greatist spoke to breathing expert Dr. Alison McConnell, yoga instructor Rebecca Pacheco and psychologist Dr. Ellen Langer. But follow closely: breathing easy isn't quite as easy as it sounds.

From the confines of a bed, a desk or anyplace where negativity finds its way, consider these six breathing techniques to help keep calm and carry on.

1. SAMA VRITTI OR *"EQUAL BREATHING"*

How it's done: Balance can do a body good, beginning with the breath. To start, inhale for a count of four, then exhale for a count of four — all through the nose, which adds a natural resistance to the breath. Got the basic <u>pranayama</u> down? More advanced yogis can aim for six to eight counts per breath with the same goal in mind: calm the nervous system, increase focus and reduce stress, Pacheco says.

When it works best: Anytime, anyplace — but this is one technique that's especially effective before bed. *"Similar to counting sheep,"* Pacheco says, *"if you're having trouble falling asleep, this breath can help take your mind off the racing thoughts, or whatever might be distracting you from sleep."*

Level of difficulty: Beginner

2. ABDOMINAL BREATHING TECHNIQUE

How it's done: With one hand on the chest and the other on the belly, take a deep breath in through the nose, ensuring the diaphragm (not the chest) inflates with enough air to create a stretch in the lungs. The goal: Six to 10 deep, slow breaths per minute for 10 minutes each day to experience immediate reductions to heart rate and blood pressure, McConnell says. Keep at it for six to eight weeks, and those benefits might stick around even longer.

When it works best: Before an exam, or any stressful event. But keep in mind, *"Those who operate in a stressed state all the time might be a little shocked how hard it is to control the* breath," Pacheco says. To help train the breath, consider biofeedback tools such as McConnell's <u>Breathe Strong app</u>, which can help users pace their breathing wherever they are.

Level of difficulty: Beginner

3. NADI SHODHANA OR *"ALTERNATE NOSTRIL BREATHING"*

How it's done: A yogi's best friend, this breath is said to bring calm and balance, and unite the right and left <u>sides of the brain</u>. Starting in a comfortable meditative pose, hold the right thumb over the right nostril and inhale deeply through the left nostril. At the peak of inhalation, close off the left nostril with the ring finger, then exhale through the right nostril. Continue the pattern, inhaling through the right nostril, closing it off with the right thumb and exhaling through the left nostril.

When it works best: Crunch time, or whenever it's time to focus or energize. Just don't try this one before bed: Nadi shodhana is said to *"clear the channels"* and make people feel more awake. *"It's almost like a cup of coffee,"* Pacheco says.

Level of difficulty: Intermediate

4. KAPALABHATI OR *"SKULL SHINING BREATH"*

How it's done: Ready to brighten up your day from the inside out? This one begins with a long, slow inhale, followed by a quick, powerful exhale generated from the lower belly. Once comfortable with the contraction, up the pace to one inhale-exhale (all through the nose) every one to two seconds, for a total of 10 breaths.

When it works best: When it's time to wake up, warm up or start looking on the brighter side of things. *"It's pretty abdominal-intensive,"* Pacheco says, *"but it will warm up the body, shake off stale energy and wake up the brain."* If alternate nostril breathing is like coffee, consider this a shot of espresso, she says.

Level of difficulty: Advanced

5. PROGRESSIVE RELAXATION

How it's done: To nix tension from head to toe, close the eyes and focus on tensing and relaxing each muscle group for two to three seconds each. Start with the feet and toes, then move up to the knees, thighs, rear, chest, arms, hands, neck, jaw and eyes — all while maintaining deep, slow breaths. Having trouble staying on track? Anxiety and panic specialist Dr. Patricia Farrell suggests we breathe in through the nose, hold for a count of five while the muscles tense, then breathe out through the mouth on release.

When it works best: At home, at a desk or even on the road. One word of caution: Dizziness is never the goal. If holding the breath ever feels uncomfortable, tone it down to just a few seconds at most.

Level of difficulty: Beginner

6. Guided Visualization

How it's done: Head straight for that *"happy place,"* no questions asked. With a coach, therapist or helpful recording as your guide, breathe deeply while focusing on pleasant, positive images to replace any negative thoughts. Psychologist Dr. Ellen Langer explains that while it's just one means of achieving mindfulness, *"Guided visualization helps put you in the place you want to be, rather than letting your mind go to the internal dialogue that is stressful."*

When it works best: Pretty much anyplace you can safely close your eyes and let go, (e.g., not at the wheel of a car.)

Level of difficulty: Intermediate

While stress, frustration, and other daily setbacks will always be there, the good news is, so will our breath.

HOW TO WRITE A HAIKU
(The Haiku Handbook by William J. Higginson)

Poetry is always an attempt to put into words what one is struggling to experience more fully. It becomes clear to the poet that the reality is deeper and beyond the words and that they are merely springboards to what rests more deeply within and is wordless. Haikus are short spurts of such words. They might be called Japanese insight poetry and a very simple way of drenching ourselves in nature. Most importantly, they have the ability to open the mind and then the heart to an encounter with the presence. To create a haiku does take a bit of discipline and exactitude.

Try writing a haiku. Simply look out your window and using details related to the senses of sight, hearing, touch, smell, or taste focus on a small detail that contains the feeling of the larger scene. Another approach is following steps below to write a *"surprise-ending haiku."*

> ➤ Write two lines about something beautiful in nature. You can use the pictures in a magazine for ideas. Don't worry about counting syllables yet.
> ➤ Write a third line that is a complete surprise, that is about something completely different from the first two lines.
> ➤ Look at the three lines together. Does the combination of these two seemingly unrelated parts suggest any surprising relationships? Does it give you any interesting ideas?

➢ Now rewrite the poem, using the 5-syllable, 7-syllable, 5-syllable format and experimenting with the new ideas or perspectives that have occurred to you.

The following are two different translations of a frog haiku by Matsuo Bashō (1644-1694)

> There is the old pond!
> Lo, into it jumps a frog:
> hark, water's music!
> (Translated by John Bryan)

> The silent old pond
> a mirror of ancient calm,
> a frog-leaps-in splash.
> (Translated by Dion O'Donnol)

You are invited to try writing a haiku as a way of being intimately present to reality and as a springboard for moving from your head to your heart, from thinking to awareness and the presence. Let the creative process be a portal to a deeper knowing, beyond definition and description to experience. Ultimately it is, as William Blake has said, *"To see a world in a grain of sand, and heaven in a wild flower."*

FRUITS OF AWARENESS

(From *The Presence Process* by Michael Brown, pp. 244-49)

1. We respond instead of reacting
2. We have more energy
3. We overcome procrastination
4. We complete tasks efficiently, effortlessly, and feel as though we have more time in which to accomplish them
5. We no longer hurry
6. Working conditions become more enjoyable
7. We are less resistant to the unpredictable currents of life
8. We experience spontaneous creativity
9. We feel more comfortable around our immediate family
10. Circumstances and people that once annoyed us no longer take up our attention
11. Our intimate relationships improve
12. We stop interfering in other people's lives
13. Our sleep is more restful
14. Nagging symptoms we may have experienced for years are integrated
15. Longtime habits cease
16. We lose weight without dieting
17. We enjoy being around children
18. We laugh more and are more playful
19. Our diet gravitates effortlessly toward eating healthily
20. We take active interest in our health
21. People are attracted to us and enjoy our company

22. We enjoy solitude
23. We sense events before they occur
24. We experience synchronicity in the events of life
25. We experience greater abundance
26. We feel less inclined to plan the future
27. We spring-clean our house and let go of "stuff" we have hoarded for years
28. We manifest less drama
29. Our outlook is naturally optimistic
30. We become interested in our vibrational wellbeing
31. We cease seeking distraction
32. We are more gentle and compassionate toward ourselves
33. We experience less anxiety
34. We are more compassionate and have more patience with others
35. Our life becomes a journey and not an intended destination
36. We experience spontaneous gratitude
37. What we require comes to us instead of our seeking it out
38. We feel a deeper sense of connection with nature
39. We become part of the natural cycles
40. We perceive the window dressing of the world
41. We no longer seek the extraordinary
42. Our capacity for trusting our insight blossoms
43. We feel blessed with purpose
44. We make an authentic contribution to this world

E

COMPARING SIMILAR EXPERIENCES OF SATISFACTION

DIRECTIONS:

➢ When describing your experience of the silence, a specific follow-up question will always be helpful. The following table offers you a way of comparing each experience of silence with a similarly described experience. In comparing the two you can then ask yourself which was more satisfying. Doing so connects your longing or yearning for deeper experiences to their respective objects. What seasoned folks who practice contemplative prayer have found is that they can then increase their motivation to follow their bliss and chose contemplation over lesser objects means of union.

➢ For example, let us say that you would describe the experience of prayer as, *"comforting and warm."* The follow-up question would be, *"How does this experience of "comforting and warm" compare with other similar experiences where you have felt the same way?"* That other experience may have been a snowy night at a ski lodge last winter or sitting in front of a fire in the fireplace at home with the family.

➢ The reason for the follow-up question is to compare how the two different experiences described by the same word or words satisfied. It is most probable that the contemplative one will have been deeper, fuller, more satisfying.

➤ If this were so, then there would be more of a tendency to return to contemplative presence the next time.

➤ What is really at work here, of course, is that the deepest longing of our hearts is being met in the divine presence and that all other similar experiences will pale by comparison.

➤ A little exercise to further study these kinds of comparisons would be to create a 5x7 table and in the first column list the mantra used for prayer, then the adjectives that describe your experience of the presence. In the third column list other physical experiences that the same adjective might describe. In the 4th column note any differences. A possible chart follows and can be copied to represent a week of comparisons.

Sacred Word(s) Mantra	Description of Experience	Prior Experience with Similar Feelings, Emotions?	Note Any Differences	Reflection on the Preference and Why?

F

WEEKLY CONTEMPLATION LOG

TRACKING OR JOURNALING

- ➢ Day 1:
    - o Choose a phrase that shimmers from your morning prayer
    - o Sit-In-Silence (S-I-S) for 5 or 10 minutes
    - o Describe the experience
    - o State an intention
    - o Live out the day, recalling the intention from time to time
- ➢ Day 2:
    - o Recall yesterday and how the intention was actually fulfilled
    - o From your morning prayer choose a phrase that shimmers
    - o Continue the steps from Day 1: Silence, Experience, Intention, and Live Out the Day

My Contemplative Living (Contemplation → Action) for the Week of _____, Page _____						
Date	Phrase That Shimmers	Sacred Word(s)	S I S	Description of the Experience	Intention (Attitudinal, General, Specific)	Action (Recorded the next morning when preparing that day's "Phrase that shimmers")
	"Surrender to God and he will give you all you need"	Surrender / receive		Trust	Remain open to whatever the Lord presents to me today (Attitudinal)	Picked up trash along the jogging route
	"Deny yourself, pick up your cross and follow me"	Deny / follow		Freedom	Prayerfully listening at our committee meeting today (General)	Was able to build on the parts of a proposal I agreed with
	"Abide in me and I in you"	Me / you		Oneness	Conversation with a friend during our drive to a meeting (Specific)	Openness to a drawn out conversation in car and over dinner

Note: Duplicate this sheet for a weekly record of tracking your contemplative actions.

Date	Phrase That Shimmers	Sacred Word(s)	S I S	Description of the Experience	Intention (Attitudinal, General, Specific)	Action (Recorded the next morning when preparing that day's "Phrase that shimmers")
My Contemplative Living (Contemplation → Action) for the Week of _____, Page ____						

BIBLIOGRAPHY

Adams, Kathleen. *Journal to the Self: Twenty-two paths to personal growth,* Warner Books, 1990.

Anonymous. *The Cloud of Unknowing,* Translated by Carmen Acevedo Butcher. Shambhala Publications, Inc., Boston, MA, 2009

Barnstone, Willis (Translator). *"The Poems of St. John of the Cross."* New Directions Publishing Corp., NY. 1972.

Brown, Michael. *The Presence Practice: A journey into present moment awareness,* Revised Edition, Namaste Publishing, Vancouver, British Columbia, 2012 (5th Printing)

DeCausade, Jean-Pierre. *Abandonment to Divine Providence.* Translated by John Beevers. Image Books, Doubleday. NY. 1975

_____. *The Sacrament of the Present Moment.* Harper and Row, 1981.

DeLeon, OSB, Roy. *Praying with the Body: Bringing the Psalms to life.* Paraclete Press, Brewster, MA. 2009.

DeMello, Anthony. *"Awareness: The perils and opportunities of reality."* Doubleday, NY. 1990.

Dougherty, Rose Mary. *Discernment: A path to spiritual awakening.* Paulist Press, NY. 2009.

Duhigg, Charles. *The Power of Habit: Why we do what we do in life and business.* Random House, NY. 2012.

Gallagher, OMV, Timothy M. *The Examen Prayer: Ignatian wisdom for our lives today.* Crossroad Publishing Company, NY. 2006.

Ganss, SJ. George (Translator). *"The Spiritual Exercises of Saint Ignatius."* The Institute of Jesuit Sources, St. Louis, MO. 1992.

Housden, Roger. *"For Lovers of God Everywhere: Poems of the Christian mystics."* Hay House, Inc. Carlsbad, CA. 2009.

Keating, Thomas. *Invitation to Love,* Bloomsbury Publishing, London. 2012.

_____. *Open Mind, Open Heart: The contemplative dimension of the Gospel.* Continuum, NY. 2008.

_____. *The Foundations for Centering Prayer and the Christian Contemplative Life.* Bloomsbury Publishing, London, 2002.

_____. *The Mystery of Christ: The liturgy as spiritual experience.* Continuum International Publishing Group, Inc., 2008.

Laird, Martin. *"Into the Silent Land: A guide to the Christians Practice of contemplation."* Oxford University Press, NY. 2006.

Martin, James. *The Jesuit Guide to (Almost) Everything: A spirituality for real life.* HarperCollins Publishers, NY. 2010.

May, Gerald. *The Dark Night of the Soul: A psychiatrist explores the connection between darkness and spiritual growth.* HarperSanFrancisco, 2004.

_____. *The Awakened Heart: Opening yourself to the love you need.* HarperSanFrancisco. 1993.

_____. *The Wisdom of the Wilderness: Experiencing the healing power of nature.* HarperSanFrancisco, 2006.

Merton, Thomas. *Contemplative Prayer.* Crown Publishing Group (Division of Random House), NY. 1969.

_____. *"In the Dark before the Dawn: New selected poems of Thomas Merton."* New Directions Publishing, NY. 2005.

Newberg, MD, and Waldman, Mark Robert. *"How God Changes Your Brain."* Ballantine Books, NY. 2009.

Oliver, Mary. *New and Selected Poems.* Beacon Press, Boston. 1992.

Rohr, Richard. *The Naked Now: Learning to see as the mystics see."* Crossroad Publishing Co., NY. 2009.

Rolheiser, Ronald. *"The Holy Longing: The search for a Christian Spirituality."* Doubleday, NY. 1999.

Ryan, Thomas. *Prayer of Heart and Body: Meditation and yoga as Christian Spiritual Practice.* Paulist Press, NJ. 1995.

Singer, Michael. *"The Untethered Soul: The journey beyond yourself."* New Harbinger Publications, Inc. Oakland, CA. 2007.

Tolle, Eckhart. *"A New Earth: Awakening to Your Life's Purpose."* Penguin Group, NY. 2005.

_____. *"The Power of Now: A guide to spiritual enlightenment."* New World Library, CA. 1999.

Waldron, Robert. *"Thomas Merton: Master of attention."* Paulist Press, NJ. 2008.